Islamization and
Activism in Malaysia

The **Strategic Information and Research Development Centre (SIRD)** is an independent publishing house founded in January 2000 in Petaling Jaya, Malaysia. The SIRD list focuses on Malaysian and Southeast Asian Studies, Economics, Gender Studies, the Social Sciences, Politics and International Relations. Our books address the scholarly community, students, the NGO and development communities, policymakers, activists and the wider public.

SIRD also distributes titles (via its sister organisation, **GB Gerakbudaya Enterprise Sdn Bhd**) published by scholarly and institutional presses, NGOs and other independent publishers. We also organise seminars, forums and group discussions. All this, we believe, is conducive to the development and consolidation of the notions of civil liberty and democracy.

The **Institute of Southeast Asian Studies (ISEAS)** was established as an autonomous organization in 1968. It is a regional centre dedicated to the study of socio-political, security and economic trends and developments in Southeast Asia and its wider geostrategic and economic environment. The Institute's research programmes are the Regional Economic Studies (RES, including ASEAN and APEC), Regional Strategic and Political Studies (RSPS), and Regional Social and Cultural Studies (RSCS).

ISEAS Publishing, an established academic press, has issued more than 2,000 books and journals. It is the largest scholarly publisher of research about Southeast Asia from within the region. ISEAS Publishing works with many other academic and trade publishers and distributors to disseminate important research and analyses from and about Southeast Asia to the rest of the world.

ISEAS Series on Islam

Islamization and Activism in Malaysia

JULIAN C.H. LEE

S

SIRD

STRATEGIC INFORMATION AND RESEARCH DEVELOPMENT CENTRE
Petaling Jaya, Malaysia

ISEAS

INSTITUTE OF SOUTHEAST ASIAN STUDIES
Singapore

First published in Singapore in 2010 by
ISEAS Publications
Institute of Southeast Asian Studies
30 Heng Mui Keng Terrace
Pasir Panjang
Singapore 119614
E-mail: publish@iseas.edu.sg
Website: http://bookshop.iseas.edu.sg

Co-published for distribution in Malaysia only by
Strategic Information and Research Development Centre
No 11, Lorong 11/4E, 46200 Petaling Jaya, Selangor, Malaysia.
E-mail: sird@streamyx.com
Website: www.gerakbudaya.com
SIRD ISBN: 978-983-3782-96-3 (Soft cover)

*The responsibility for facts and opinions in this publication rests exclusively with the
author and his interpretations do not necessarily reflect the views or the policy of the
publishers or their supporters.*

ISEAS Library Cataloguing-in-Publication Data

Lee, Julian C. H.
   Islamization and activism in Malaysia / Julian C. H. Lee.
   1. Islam and civil society—Malaysia.
   2. Islam and states—Malaysia.
   3. Islam and politics—Malaysia.
   I. Title.
BP173.63 L47   2010

ISBN 978-981-230-838-2 (Soft cover)
ISBN 978-981-4279-02-9 (Hard cover)
ISBN 978-981-4279-03-1 (E-book PDF)

Typeset by International Typesetters Pte Ltd
Printed in Singapore by Utopia Press Pte Ltd

Dedicated to the memory of
ZAITUN "TONI" KASIM

CONTENTS

ACKNOWLEDGEMENTS

There are many people whom I must thank for their various forms of assistance during the creation of this book. I would like to thank Douglas Lewis, Andrew Dawson, Anthony Marcus, Thomas Reuter, and two anonymous reviewers for their comments on drafts of this text. I would also like to thank Richard Sutcliffe, Claire Knowles, Simone Blair, and Tanya King, who amongst other things, commented on chapters of this book.

There are many people in Malaysia I must thank for their assistance in my research. Amongst these are Abdul Mohaimin Ayus, Abdul Rahman Othman, Ann James, Augustine Julian, Chua Siew Eng, Edmund Bon, Elizabeth Wong, Eric Paulsen, Haris bin Mohamed Ibrahim, Irene Xavier, Jahaberdeen YM Mohamed Yunoos, Khalid Jaafar, Kua Kia Soong, Latheefa Koya, Leonard Teoh, Malik Imtiaz Sarwar, Moganambal Murugappan, Masjaliza Hamzah, Mustapha Ma, S. Nagarajan, Norani Othman, Norhayati Kaprawi, Father O.C. Lim, P. Uthayakumar, Patricia Martinez, Salbiah Ahmad, Shanon Shah, Sharmila Sekaran, Sivarasa Rasiah, Sonia Randhawa, Sumit Mandal, Syed Husin Ali, Said Zahari, Xavier Jayakumar, Yeoh Seng Guan and Zaitun "Toni" Kasim. Thanks must also go to the staff of Daim and Gamany (advocates and solicitors), Sisters in Islam, Suara Rakyat Malaysia, and these organizations' staff for the various forms of assistance they kindly gave to me.

Thanks must go to my parents Lee Eng Hua and Barbara Lee and likewise must I thank my brother Marcus and his wife Elizabeth Miller. And thanks are also owed to Sarah Thwaites for her editorial assistance and all the support and encouragement needed for completing this book.

The completion of this book was made possible by a Fellowship from the Economic and Social Research Council (U.K.) which I spent in the School of Anthropology and Conservation, University of Kent in 2009. The initial research was made possible by an Australian Postgraduate Award that supported me throughout my Ph.D. studies which I undertook at the School of Anthropology, Geography and Environmental Studies, University of Melbourne between 2003 and 2006. Subsequent research was undertaken in 2007 and 2008 while I was a lecturer in the School of Arts and Social Sciences, Monash University, and in 2009, while a fellow at the International Institute of Asian Studies (IIAS). My thanks go to all the institutions that supported me in the course of the making of this book. Thanks also go to *Südostasian Aktuell* for permission to reprint portions of my article, "Barisan Nasional Political Dominance and the General Elections of 2004 in Malaysia" (no. 2 [2007]: 39–66). These portions appear in Chapters 2 and 8 of this book.

ABBREVIATIONS

BN	Barisan Nasional (National Front)
DAP	Democratic Action Party
HINDRAF	Hindu Rights Action Force
HSLU	Harmonisation of Shari'ah and Law Unit
ISA	Internal Security Act
JAKIM	Jabatan Kemajuan Islam Malaysia (Department of Islamic Development Malaysia)
JAWI	Jabatan Agama Islam Wilayah Persekutuan (Federal Territory Islamic Department)
MCA	Malaysian Chinese Association
NGO	Non-government organization (also known as a civil society organization)
NRD	National Registration Department
PACA	Polling Agent/Counting Agent
PAS	Parti Islam SeMalaysia
PKR	Parti Keadilan Rakyat
SB	Special Branch (of the police)
SIS	Sisters in Islam
UMNO	United Malays National Organization
WCI	Women's Candidacy Initiative

INTRODUCTION

CIVIL SOCIETY, DEMOCRACY, AND
THE PUBLIC SPHERE(S) IN MALAYSIA

This book is concerned with civil society's reactions to some of the negative impacts of political, legal, and social Islamization in Malaysia. I examine how different groups of people in Malaysia have sought to counter threats to the public domain and to their civil liberties as a result of authoritarianism, especially when it is linked to social, political, and legal Islamization. I examine the challenges that members of civil society face in engaging in their work in Malaysia and I also describe the various ways that activists seek to overcome the challenges they encounter. I try to illuminate the creative ways in which members of civil society both make use of existing public spaces and seek to create new spaces.

The scholarly interest in civil society outside the West is linked to the positive correlation that is perceived to exist between civil society and democracy. Democracy — and more specifically, liberal democracy — is now the normative form of government, and the extent to which States deviate from the ideal of liberal democracy is the extent to which they are frequently regarded by scholars and other governments as deficient. To the end of judging the state of democracy in a given country, the health of its civil society is often regarded as a key indicator. Civil society and democracy are often regarded as mutually supporting if not mutually causal.

1

What constitutes civil society is, however, difficult to pin down. There are contemporary and classical ideas about what civil society is. But as Salvador Gilner notes, there is even "no such thing as the classical conception of civil society" as there are, among others, the Lockean, Hegelian, Hobbesian, Marxian and Gramscian understandings of it (1995, p. 304).

Some, however, might call for caution in using "civil society" altogether in trying to understand subaltern or counter-hegemonic politics in Malaysia. Owing to the impreciseness of "civil society" even when confined to describing a European phenomenon, some authors have suggested that civil society is a concept that scholars should be all the more wary of when using in Asian contexts. Wayne Hudson notes that whereas "civil society" was a term that was developed *after* the phenomenon it described came into being in Western contexts, in Asia, that which it is supposed to denote is still developing (Hudson 2003, p. 15). Perhaps a better caution is to be aware of the fact that civil society and democracy alike are ideas that are descriptive in some instances, prescriptive in others, and simultaneously both descriptive and prescriptive in yet others. Indeed, while recognizing the flaws in the concept of civil society, John L. Comaroff and Jean Comaroff, while writing with regard to Africa, also recognize that civil society "serves, almost alone in the age of neoliberal capital, to give shape to reformist, even utopian visions" (1999, p. 33).

> In short, in Africa as in other places, "civil society" evokes a polythetic clutch of signs. An all-purpose placeholder, it captures otherwise inchoate — as yet unnamed and unnameable — popular aspirations, moral concerns, sites and spaces of practice; likewise, it bespeaks a scholarly effort to recalibrate worn-out methodological tools, and to find a positive politics, amid conceptual confusion (ibid, p. 3).

Given the polythetic nature of "civil society", the contribution that anthropology can make to its study is, as Chris Hann has noted, to be

> concerned with analogues to the discourse in non-European cultural traditions, and with the interaction of these specific cultural ideas with the putative universalism of civil society as this idea is exported across the globe. Ethnographic research would focus on how these ideas are manifested in practice, in everyday social behaviour (1996, p. 2).

The focus then of this book is on three distinct but overlapping realms of civil society activism in Kuala Lumpur, Malaysia. These realms are the law, social activism (including progressive Islamic activism), and elections. Those who I describe in the following chapters work in a country that is recognized by commentators as authoritarian and in a socio-political climate tending towards Islamic primacy and conservatism. I describe the various discourses they deploy and fields of action they engage to gainsay constrictions of the public domain that are linked to the effects of this Islamization. I examine the work they do (and the context in which they do it) through analyses of particular campaigns, issues and court cases.

In different ways, these campaigns contest the marginalization of the (conflated) non-Malay and non-Muslim segments of the Malaysian population. However, concomitant with, if not central to, this marginalization, is the electoral and therefore parliamentary control that the Barisan Nasional (BN, or National Front) coalition, which is dominated by the United Malays National Organisation (UMNO), has enjoyed for much of Malaysia's history. Almost uninterrupted between Malaysia's independence in 1957 through to 2008, the BN had a two-thirds majority in Parliament which allowed it to make laws and amend the Constitution, often in its own self-interest and to the detriment of civil liberties, civil society, and democracy in its broader sense. This power had also enabled UMNO to infuse the Constitution and government policies with an Islamic presence in order to meet what it perceives as the demands of its Muslim-Malay constituency.

The particular concern that this book has with erosions to civil liberties that emanate from political Islam sheds light on concerns that researchers into civil society have held with regard to Islam per se. John A. Hall, for instance, regards the salutary effects of civil society as being by no means latent in every society. Along with the caste system in India, Hall regards Islam as having a problematic relationship with civil society. He writes that

> current history makes it absolutely apparent that Islam possesses a civilisational vision of its own, radically opposed to that of the West. The logical clarity enshrined in Islam — the monistic and puritanical scriptualism of its monotheism — obviated any equivalent to occidental "liberties" ... (1995, p. 14).

Indeed, Islam is sometimes seen as antithetical to civil society. "Islamic ideals", write Comaroff and Comaroff, "are often seen as sinister inversions of modernity: as irrational, imperialist, fundamentalist" (1999, p. 28). These latter characteristics are thought to stifle discussion and reduce the variety of publically presentable opinions. They are deleterious to the openness of the public sphere which, in Jürgen Habermas's conception, is characterized by open and rational discursive deliberation (Habermas 1992).

Habermas's work on the public sphere has profoundly shaped discussions and understandings of what constitutes civil society. Michael E. Gardiner concisely summarizes Habermas's idea thus:

[I]n the eighteenth and nineteenth centuries, a distinct forum for rational public debate emerged in most Western European countries. It constituted an area of social life, separate from the state apparatus, in which citizens gathered to converse about issues of the day in a free and unrestricted fashion, either literally, as in the town square, or in the pages of diverse journals and periodicals. Debate proceeded according to universal standards of critical reason and argumentative structure that all could recognise and assent to; appeals to traditional dogmas, or to arbitrary subjective prejudices, were ruled inadmissible. Thus, it was in the public sphere that "discursive will formation" was actualized in a manner that represented the general social interest, as opposed to a class or sectional one (Gardiner 2004, p. 28).

Habermas's notion of the public sphere as it ought to be has, however, been criticized from a number of quarters. One eminent critique comes from Nancy Fraser. While admitting that Habermas's public sphere is needed in social theory, Fraser points to the work of others who argue that, contrary to Habermas's reckoning, it is highly exclusive and not a forum whereat all members of the public can have their voices heard as equals with their differences bracketed out and made irrelevant. Habermas's public sphere was (as Habermas identifies) bourgeois and (as Habermas neglects to identify) masculine (1990, p. 59).

After noting the error in Habermas's idea that all members of the public could participate in the public sphere as equals, Fraser goes on to note that the notion of the single public sphere is also in error. While there may have been a dominant public sphere, there were also other competing public spheres. Examples include women-only voluntary associations in America. While these associations were in many ways similar to men's organizations, they also differed in that "they creatively used the heretofore quintessentially 'private' idioms of domesticity and motherhood precisely as springboards for public activity" (ibid., p. 61).

Thus, rather than a single bourgeois, rational and masculine public sphere, there was always "a multiplicity of public arenas" and "the bourgeois public was never *the* public" (ibid.). These subordinate or subaltern publics are referred to by Fraser as counterpublics and these counterpublics have always contested the exclusiveness of the dominant bourgeois public.

Among her arguments, Fraser asserts that viewing the public domain as constituted by numerous public spheres is more productive than viewing it as composed of one Habermasian public sphere. She argues that "arrangements that accommodate contestation among a plurality of competing publics better promote the ideal of participatory parity than does a single, comprehensive, overarching public" (ibid., p. 66).

An issue that Fraser is unable to resolve, however, is the means by which competing publics engage with each other on issues of mutual relevance. While noting that "the discursive relations among differently empowered publics are as likely to take the form of contestation as that of deliberation" (ibid., p. 68), she asks how the public domain may be structured such that debating publics "share enough in the way of values, expressive norms, and, therefore, protocols of persuasion to lend their talk the quality of deliberations aimed at reaching agreement through giving reasons?" (ibid., p. 69). While seeing no in-principle reason to suggest that such a medium was impossible, Fraser concludes that the question is better treated as an empirical question rather than a conceptual one (ibid.).

It is here that my ethnographic work with activists helps to shed light on how competing civil society publics engage with each other and the State in pushing forward their agendas. In post-independence Malaysia, which was ruled by a more-or-less secular (though by no means unethnicized) authoritarian government, Islamic reform movements (counterpublics) acted in Malaysia as they had in Africa, to "promote an alternative moral order" (Comaroff and Comaroff 1999, p. 29). Where ordinary secular means of finding redress for injustices and dissatisfactions were inefficacious, Islam provided another way of expressing grievances and seeking redress.

In understanding why Islam came to play this role in Malaysia, it is worth noting that Alfred Schutz has described people as located, at any given moment, within a biographically determined situation. This situation

> includes certain possibilities of future practical or theoretical activities which shall be briefly called the "purpose at hand." It is this purpose at hand which defines those elements among all the others contained in such a situation which are relevant for this purpose (1970, p. 73).

A given problem will sometimes point to a number of different ways in which the problem can be addressed. If, for example, someone were to take a possession of a sibling without consent, the aggrieved can seek redress by, among other things, calling the police, using mutual family members to intervene, or perhaps appealing to the sibling's conscience by referring to principles found within a shared religion. Which course of action the sibling will use will depend on his/her particular biographical history and personal competencies.

Similarly, Malaysian citizens have had at their disposal an array of means by which they can attempt to find redress for various injustices and dissatisfactions that emanate (or seem to emanate) from State activity. A popular course for Malaysian Muslims, for example, has been to engage in Islamic discourses and fields of action. James C. Scott has described the response of poorer Malay peasants in a Malay village where he did fieldwork when wealthier landowners began to ignore their ritual duty of distributing tithes to the poor as the latter became increasingly unnecessary to production through industrialization. "Lacking the economic or coercive sanctions to influence the behavior of the wealthy, they must necessarily turn to less mundane forms of persuasion", namely reminding the wealthy of their Islamic duties (1988, p. 206).

For those wishing to challenge authoritarianism in both its Islamic and non-Islamic expressions, realms of action available to Malaysians include the law, social activism, and elections. Activists in Kuala Lumpur who make use of these three areas are the focus of this book.

ISLAM, CIVIL SOCIETY, AND ACTIVISM IN MALAYSIA

As noted before, Islam has provided an idiom through which grievances can be aired. It has moral authority and popular traction that the government can neither ignore nor deny. In turn, the Malaysian government has co-opted this idiom and refracted its actions through it to neutralize the efficacy of criticisms articulated in the language of Islam. However, in so doing, the BN government appears to have sanctioned a conservative form of public Islam in its attempt to prove its Islamic credentials in word and deed.

The politicization of Islam in Malaysia has had legal effects. Since the introduction of English common law in Malaysia, there have also been Syariah laws that apply to Muslims and which pertain to so-called personal and family matters. However, non-Muslims are being increasingly affected by what some regard as an unwarranted intrusion by Islam into, and precedence over, civil and constitutional law. Indeed, in contests over whether a matter ought to be decided under Syariah law or civil law, it is to Syariah courts that the civil courts increasingly defer. Islam is in some ways beginning to form the underlying framework of Malaysia's socio-political and public life and the ascent of political Islam compounds some of the problems that social and political activists have always experienced as subaltern publics. In this book I describe some of the main flashpoints between Islamists and activists whose orientation is towards a liberally construed Constitution.

My concerns in this book are primarily with actors and groups who engage with the State and its different apparatuses. I have focused on those who interact with the State because State apparatuses and associated actors are a predominating avenue for the realization and legitimization of various forms of repression, including that which occurs in the name of Islam. The Malaysian State has become adept at restricting and managing interaction between activists and the populace. People's behaviours — from public assembly to personal relations — are susceptible to interference from State apparatuses as many restrictions on expression and behaviour generally have been legally codified and are enforced (albeit often arbitrarily). Indeed, a good deal of the contest between liberal constitutionalists and Islamists is related to legal matters and is contested in court, an important limb of the State.

The ethnographic data that informs this book was collected during fieldwork conducted intermittently between late 2003 and mid-2008. I collected my data primarily by participating in and observing the activities of different kinds of activists in Kuala Lumpur, and as such this book is concerned with events in and the politics of West or peninsular Malaysia. The activists with whom I worked can, for the most part, be broadly broken down into three main types. The first were lawyers, the second were non-government organization-related activists, and the third were political party members — for the most part from Parti Keadilan Rakyat (PKR, or People's Justice Party).

No observer of or researcher into Malaysian politics and activism can deny the important presence of Islam. As I intimated above, Islam has been a repository of ethical axioms for criticizing the government in terms that the government cannot easily dismiss. Political Islam in Malaysia is thus in accord with Raymond Firth's note that

> [a] religion can then offer a revolutionary alternative to an established political system such as that which would define the relative powers of church and state. More generally, it might be argued that some of the most important religious movements, at their beginning, have been as much challenges to the established order as escapes from it (1996, p. 66).

However, as will be seen, politicized Islam is, in the view of many, an ambiguous ally in gainsaying political repression. In Malaysia, there are now issues of considerable importance relating to the place of Islam in the nation and to Islamically founded restrictions on individual freedoms.

OVERVIEW

In Chapter 1, I contextualize my discussion of authoritarianism, Islam, and activism within larger discussions about Islam, democracy, and civil society. I also explain why Malaysia provides a good case to examine to draw out issues pertaining to the relationship between Islam, democracy, and activism. Also in Chapter 1, I examine the role that activists and political vanguards play in bringing about social change and in widening democracy.

In Chapter 2, I begin my examination of the Malaysian context of authoritarianism, Islam, and activism by providing a brief political history of Malaysia. I touch only on those events that provide a pertinent background for the issues dealt with in this book, but also examine some important features of the Malaysian national narrative and their impacts, in particular the 13 May 1969 riots and Malay political dominance.

In Chapters 3, 4, and 5, I examine the legal consequences of, and the reactions to, the politically legitimized construal of Malaysia as an Islamic state. In 2001 then Prime Minister Mahathir Mohamad announced that Malaysia was an Islamic state. This was a self-confessed manoeuvre to take the wind out of the sails of opposition Islamic party PAS (Parti Islam se-Malaysia, or Islamic Party of Malaysia) which advocated turning Malaysia into an Islamic state. However, in the view of many, the ramifications of this announcement have reached far and the debate that followed was no mere war of words. The announcement lent legitimacy and consequently political efficacy to Islamists who advocated implementing what were said to be the legitimate demands of Islam. In the views of these Islamists, it is the duty of an Islamic government to institute Syariah law completely, at least for Muslims, in a Muslim majority country such as Malaysia.

In Chapter 3, I examine three perspectives regarding the place of Islam in Malaysia. These three perspectives emanate from UMNO, a liberal constitutionalist lawyer, and PAS. I describe how both UMNO and PAS conceive of Malaysia as an Islamic state in very different ways and the view of many activists in Kuala Lumpur who believe Islam's social and political role has exceeded its constitutional limits.

In Chapter 4, I examine the legal case of a Malay woman, born of Muslim parents, who has accepted the Christian faith and wished to marry a Christian man. She was, however, prevented from marrying this man unless she could officially convert out of Islam or unless he converted to Islam. I examine the arguments put to the presiding judges by her counsel and the counsel for the Islamic Council of the Federal Territory. The latter sought to assert restrictions on the movement of people from Islam. The relevance of this to a discussion of civil society is clear as freedom of association and conscience is often regarded as critical to a properly functioning civil society. Orthodox Islamic notions that regard apostasy as impossible, criminal, and/or punishable, challenge this aspect of civil society and put into question Islam's commensurability with civil society and democracy.

The political positions that give rise to the arguments of both sides are at the heart of a more general contest in the wider socio-political environment. First, at stake is the place — integral or peripheral — of Malaysia's substantial non-Muslim population in the nation's image of itself. If construed as peripheral, this will bear upon the political efficacy of non-Muslims in the public domain. Second, at stake are the rights of Muslims within Malaysia to practise their faith according to their personal beliefs and consciences which may differ from what is sanctioned by the State.

Whereas in Chapter 4, I pay greater attention to lawyers who defend a liberal interpretation of the Constitution, in Chapter 5, I focus on some Islamist lawyers' views. These are the perspectives of three lawyers who defend positions that I would describe as giving Islam and Islamic law primacy in Malaysia. One lawyer whose writings I examine is the late Ahmad Mohamed Ibrahim. His work exerts continuing influence on legal thinking in Malaysia and his thoughts on the constitutional place of Islam are an example of the more technical legal reasoning displayed by Islamist lawyers. Through my examination I point out a significant difference in how Syariah law is imagined in comparison to civil law.

Chapter 6 begins with the reactions of some actors and groups to the Islamists' agenda. Whereas the preceding chapters will have paid closer attention to the legal ramifications of Islamization in Malaysia, in Chapter 6, I examine the result of the realization among some lawyers and activists that legal redress is inadequate without engaging in a simultaneous public campaign. I describe the coalition they formed and their campaign to protect freedom of religion. In so doing, I also describe some of the extant consequences that restrictions on religious freedom have for Malaysians.

In Chapter 7, I examine some of the wider socio-political dynamics of Islamic activism and political Islam in Malaysia. In particular I describe the work of the Malaysian Muslim women's non-government organization (NGO), Sisters in Islam. With this description I account for the important work done by one NGO that works within the framework of Islam.

Thus far in this book, I have examined some different ways in which activists and groups work in order to advance their agendas. The fields of action have included the law, Islam, and social activism. In Chapter 8, I examine the role that Malaysia's particular democratic system has played in facilitating the Islamization described in this book. I discuss how, given the legitimacy that this system lends to both authoritarianism generally and Islamization in particular, activists have engaged with it. Some activists have made use of political parties as vehicles for seeking redress while others have sought to reform the electoral system.

While this book does attempt to give a grounded description of activism in Kuala Lumpur in the face of authoritarianism and Islamization, it does not attempt to be exhaustive. However, the larger issues pertaining to authoritarianism and the impact of Islamization which I do describe will find resonance well beyond Kuala Lumpur. Indeed, given, for example, the worldwide coverage of *fatwas* delivered in Malaysia against yoga and tomboys in late 2008, and that Malaysia is seen by many as a model nation that is successfully combining Islam with modernity (for example, El-Affendi 2008, p. 33), the wider relevance of this examination beyond Kuala Lumpur is considerable.

1

ON ISLAM, DEMOCRACY, AND ACTIVISM

WHY MALAYSIA?

Malaysia recapitulates some global trends and issues relating to the management of national, ethnic, and religious sentiments. One current issue, both in Malaysia and on the world stage, is Islam's putative intolerance of what are for some basic political freedoms. The "cartoon row" that emerged in 2005 typifies some of this. Although the initial Danish context had its own complexity (see Linde-Laursen 2007), the "cartoon row", which began with a depiction of the Prophet Muhammad as a terrorist, was experienced by many Muslims as demonstrating the West's continuing and flagrant disrespect of them and their religion, albeit under the banner of the Western secular value of freedom of expression. As Karen Armstrong suggests, "fearful of the hostility in Europe and bombarded with images from Guantanamo Bay and Abu Ghraib, many [Muslims] experienced the gratuitous vilification of their prophet as the last straw" (2006).

With distinct similarities to the affair over Salman Rushdie's *The Satanic Verses* (for discussions, see Armstrong 1993 passim; Asad 1990), many in Western countries regarded the apparent reaction of Muslims as an unwarranted imposition of their religious beliefs on others. The popular commentator and author Christopher Hitchens, for example, criticized the U.S. State Department for denouncing the cartoons that sparked the riots.

Acknowledging the prohibitions that many Muslims have on depicting their prophet, and on drinking alcohol and eating pork, Hitchens writes, "let a good Muslim abstain rigorously from all these. But if he claims the right to make me abstain as well, he offers the clearest possible warning and proof of an aggressive intent" (Hitchens 2006). A (secular) civil society means, Hitchens continues, "that free expression trumps the emotions of anyone to whom free expression might be inconvenient".

In Malaysia demands for freedoms and liberties are often denied on the grounds that Muslims' sensitivities must be respected. Most Muslims are ethnic Malays who, along with (non-Malay) indigenous Malaysians are termed *bumiputera* (sons of the soil). As of 2007, Malays made up just over 50 per cent of Malaysia's population of 27 million, but *bumiputera* altogether made up just over 60 per cent (see Syed H.A. 2008*a*, p. 202).

During the British colonial period, large numbers of mostly non-Muslim Chinese and Indian immigrants arrived in Malaysia. As of 2007, Chinese constituted just over 23 per cent of the population, and Indians just under 8 per cent (ibid.). As I demonstrate later, contemporary inter-ethnic tensions come to be refracted through the prism of religion with calls for the (largely non-Muslim) Chinese and Indian populations to respect Muslim sensitivities. This in effect affirms Muslim-Malay political precedence.

The government often censors discussion of issues relating to the practice of Islam, especially when they are raised by non-Muslims, and even when it impacts on their lives. The construction and naming of churches, for instance, has often been obstructed out of ostensible concern for Muslim sensitivities. Likewise impeded on these grounds has, for example, been dog ownership by the non-Muslim neighbours of Muslims (owing to the belief among many Muslims that dogs are polluting).

The conservative views of some Muslims in Europe have led to public reactions against Islam's apparent socially repressive dictates. Islam has been seen as a challenge to Dutch values in the famously laissez-faire Netherlands for example. In ostensible defence of Dutch values which include gender equality and the separation of church and State, the *niqaab* (which covers all of the face except the eyes) has been banned in Amsterdam high schools (Lunsing 2003). In France more famously, the assertion of the primacy of secularism has similarly led to the veil being restricted in schools. Thus the religious liberties of Muslims have likewise been restricted in the name of secular values which attempt to make religion irrelevant in favour of national identification.

In Malaysia, however, freedom of expression, assembly, association, and even religious practice, have all been cited as issues relevant not only to national values, but also to national security. The emotional and conflictual nature of some issues has legitimized government management and interdiction of possibly incendiary behaviours. On occasion, and some would argue arbitrarily and self-servingly, the government has cracked down on various expressions of these liberties. Perhaps the most notable occasion of this was "Operasi Lalang" (Operation Weed) in 1987 in which 107 people were arrested under the Internal Security Act (ISA) (see below) ostensibly for "inflaming sentiments" and "exploiting sensitive issues" (Kua 2005, p. 94; see also Lee 2008*b*). More recently a rally in Kuala Lumpur of some 30,000 ethnic Indians saw a heavy-handed reponse from the police who used tear-gas and water-cannons on the ralliers. Furthermore, numerous leaders of the Hindu Rights Action Force (HINDRAF) were detained without trial under the ISA and dozens of ralliers were charged with the attempted murder of police (but later released without charge; for more see Chapter 8).

The theme of sacrificing individual liberties or freedoms in favour of national or global security has been an increasingly familiar one around the world, especially during George W. Bush's Presidency of the United States of America. Democratic countries and countries with pretences to democracy must justify the denial of rights that are often constitutionally enshrined by application to a prevailing condition of emergency. The 11 September 2001 terrorist attacks provided such a proximate cause for the introduction of the Patriot Act in the United States of America. Malaysia, however, has been in an official state of emergency since race riots in 1969. When there is a state of emergency in Malaysia, Clause 6 of Article 150 of the Malaysian Constitution allows laws to be made that are contradictory to the Constitution. This includes those articles relating to fundamental liberties (Wu 1999, p. 261). Although local politicians frequently proclaim that contemporary Malaysia is a model of inter-ethnic harmony, the 1969 proclamation of emergency continues.

Although not strictly an emergency power, the ISA enables the detention of persons without trial for renewable periods of two years so long as the Home Minister is satisfied that the person poses a threat to internal security. No evidence need be adduced in support of the assertion of the Minister who in recent history has often also been the Prime Minister. Probably the most well-known instance of its use was by former Prime Minister Mahathir Mohamad against former Deputy Prime Minister Anwar Ibrahim in 1998 (although Anwar was subsequently formally charged; for more see Chapter 2). The background to the creation of this Act in 1960 was an ongoing communist insurgency. However, even though the insurgency has long since faded, the ISA remains. The threat of Islamic terrorism is sometimes now used to justify its continuance and the courts have found that, contrary to some lawyers' arguments, its use is not limited to communist insurgencies (Bari and Shuaib 2004, pp. 282–83).

The ongoing use of emergency powers and the ISA predictably retards meaningful democratization in Malaysia. For Norani Othman, the threat and use of these powers are evidence of a general "ISA mentality" in the government (Norani 2004, p. 128). One might describe this mentality as one which regards serious discursive engagement in debate and deliberation with non-ruling party actors as ultimately unnecessary given that the protection of programmes or positions of the government can be secured, ostensibly in the interest of national security, through the use of repressive mechanisms.

Norani notes that this ISA mentality is also apparent in the country's Islamic bureaucracy. "Muslim deviants", defined by the Jabatan Kemajuan Islam Malaysia (Department of Islamic Development Malaysia) as those who propagate "incorrect Islamic teachings", face being sent to rehabilitation (I describe in Chapter 5 the case of a woman and three men who experienced this). The vague attributes of "deviants", Norani notes, "could easily be misused to silence discussion and debate of the legal or religious measures introduced by the state" (ibid.). Despite boasting that, unlike in Christianity, Islam has no clergy, some Muslim groups and individuals attempt to curtail debate on matters relating to Islam, usually citing scholarship in Islam as a necessary prerequisite to the right to speak about Islam. Such censorship has been advocated by orthodox authorities, government departments, members of UMNO and PAS, and members of other Islamic associations. Books addressing Islamic issues are also regularly banned and have included works by scholars Karen Armstrong and John Esposito, as well as a book published by the progressive Muslim women's NGO, Sisters in Islam, titled *Muslim Women and the Challenge of Islamic Extremism.*

Such is the official hostility towards diversity of opinion in Islam that in most Malaysian states, any Muslim who "gives, propagates or disseminates any opinion concerning Islamic teachings, Islamic Law or any issue, contrary to any fatwa … shall be guilty of offence", as it is put in the 1996 Federal Territories Syariah Criminal Offences Bill.

ISLAMIZATION AND DEMOCRACY

Especially since 11 September 2001, Islam and Muslim politics have entered something of a critical spotlight (Hefner 2005, p. 2; Volpi and Cavatorta

2006, p. 363). Indeed, Islam's compatibility with democracy and modernity has been doubted. Salim Mansur writes that,

> From Algeria to Indonesia, from Central Asian republics to Sudan, the entire Muslim world has retreated from meeting the challenge of modernity and has turned its back on modernity (2005, p. 68).

Similarly, Lauren Langman has suggested that Islamic societies have failed "to embrace the Enlightenment, especially in the Arab world" and that this "has led some to a fervent embrace of anti modernity, a dialectic of unenlightenment" (2005, p. 246).

Frédéric Volpi and Francesco Cavatorta have noted that the lack of democracy in much of the Muslim world has been a source of academic and policy-orientated debate (2006, p. 363). In examining the relationship between democracy and Islam, Volpi and Cavatorta suggest shifting "the focus away from grand culture-based explanations of democratization in the Muslim world" and towards "the practical dilemmas of political Islam and democracy" (ibid., p. 364). This book is such an examination of the situated socio-political dynamics of Islam in a democracy. I demonstrate how some actors wish to advance the social and legal Islamization of Malaysia as well as describe the arguments and manoeuvres of others in attempting to counter repressive and exclusionary expressions of Islam.

Observing in the 1960s the conservative Islam incipient in newly independent Malaysia, Gordon P. Means predicted that "[e]ventually Islam will be challenged by those members of the Muslim community who are already secular, pragmatic, and rationalist in their outlook, attitudes, and behaviour" (1969, p. 283). At the time of his writing, Means could not have known when this might occur. Much of what follows in fact deals with such challenges in the form of movements to countervail Islamist interpretations of Malaysian law and the national ascendancy of Islam.

The political role that Islam plays in Malaysia has been frequently noted by researchers. Means' earlier comments point to its presence shortly after independence in 1957 and scholars have referred to Islamic resurgences at various times in Malaysia. Ozay Mehmet describes such a resurgence in Malaysia beginning in the 1970s. This resurgence was linked to the urbanization of Malays, the activities of Angkatan Belia Islam Malaysia (ABIM, or Muslim Youth Movement of Malaysia), and the Islamic revolution in Iran (Mehmet 1990, pp. 109–10). Chandra Muzaffar points to other causes for this resurgence. Foremost among these are industrialization and urbanization. "The urban-industrial society consciously or unconsciously worships the machine and the techniques of production that accompany it"

(Muzaffar 1986, p. 65). Along with this, "the modern city tends to create a spiritual vacuum in man. It pushes man to the abyss of a lonely, atomized existence" (ibid.). Islamization then, for Muzaffar, filled this spiritual vacuum as society transformed after independence.

In 1982 Judith Nagata wrote of this 1970s resurgence being Malaysia's second "Islamic revival", the first having occurred in the 1920s and 1930s (1982, pp. 43–44). Shamsul Amri Baharuddin has criticized Nagata, however, and suggested that "Islamic revivalism" is by no means new (1983, p. 400).

> It is clear that "Islamic revival" has occurred frequently in Malaysian history. In fact, it is a misnomer to call it "revivalism" when it occurs at such regular intervals. What is actually being revived here is, in effect, foreign scholars' interest in studying Islam (ibid.).

Nevertheless, political and religious discourses do, as Shamsul admits (ibid., p. 401), act as ideological tools. The relationships that people have with ideologies, discourses, and symbols evolve with contexts over time and can be made to serve new ends. The modified manifestations of a discourse and its updated situation with other discourses and practices may well revive it, and I would suggest this is worthy of continued study.

In the year before Nagata elicited Shamsul's criticisms, Mahathir Mohamad became Prime Minister of Malaysia. Under Mahathir, Osman Bakar writes, "we witnessed the biggest and most significant Islamic transformations of the country" (2003, p. 133). It was with Mahathir that Islam became especially concerning for non-Muslims and liberal and unorthodox Muslims. This is owing to Islam's incorporation into and influence on State infrastructure and law (Noor 2003, p. 206).

In rhetoric and practice, Mahathir tried to forge a relationship between Islam and normative notions of modernity and progress. In his words, his aim was "to make Islam in Malaysia synonymous with economic progress" (quoted in Osman 2003, p. 134). But at the same time, a conflation between an Islamic agenda and a Malay agenda is apparent. Osman writes that for Mahathir, "it is only through Islam, and thus his Islamization policy that the Malays can successfully arise to the call of economic progress and modernisation" (ibid.).

We can now begin to see something of the situational complex that must be considered when speaking of the relationship between Islam and democracy. In Malaysia, advancing the Islamic agenda, in effect, advances a Malay agenda, and ethnic politics has dominated Malaysian politics before and since independence. As others have noted, while other markers of

Malay ethnicity such as language have faded in their specificity, Islam has remained a positive correlate of Malayness (Mauzy and Milne 1983–84, p. 632; Nagata 1997). Given that political Islam has often developed in a pre-existing milieu of ethnic division and authoritarianism, we should not attribute exclusivism and authoritarianism to Islam per se. I am not suggesting that Islam, like most religions, is free of illiberal idioms, but it certainly has its fair share of liberal and inclusive idioms as well. Those which come to the fore and those which recede are matters of circumstance and choices within circumstance.

An example from the Balkans illustrates how a less exclusive and less politicized Islam arises out of circumstance. Xavier Bougarel has outlined how the political situation of Balkan Muslims has led many of them to resist formulations of ethnicity and their nation that give primacy to Islamic identity. This is in contrast to identity processes in Western Europe. Bougarel notes that

> in the Balkans, the creation of nation states is still an ongoing process, whilst in Western Europe, European integration favours the emergence of a multicultural or even a transnational definition of the political community. Religious actors and symbols therefore play a very different role in the mobilisation of Muslim populations. In Western Europe, the defence of common claims favours a rapprochement between mono-ethnic religious associations. In the Balkans, Islamic religious institutions are destabilised by the strengthening of distinct ethnic and national identities (2005, p. 22).

Among non-Turkish speaking Balkan Muslims, an emergent Turkish national identity and a need to legitimize their presence in the post-Ottoman Balkans led them "to stop defining themselves as 'Turks' in the Ottoman (religious) sense of the term and, rather, to stress their indigenous nature and their pre-Ottoman past" (ibid., p. 10).

Bougarel also notes that "various rules of 'good neighbourliness' and heterodox religious practices reflect centuries of co-existence between Muslims and non-Muslims". However, the softening of the boundaries between Muslims and non-Muslims, the adoption of dietary practices contrary to Islamic orthodoxy (such as consuming pork and alcohol), and the consigning of religion to the private sphere were "not the result of five centuries of Ottoman tradition, but rather five decades of Communist moderation" (ibid., p. 11).

Along with other examples (such as Islam in South Africa, see Moosa 2000–01, pp. 211–14) the Balkan example illustrates that the characteristics of identities, ideologies, or religions are greatly influenced by circumstance and not determined by any logic or essence.

WHAT IS FUNDAMENTALISM?
WHO ARE THE FUNDAMENTALISTS?

A few words seem appropriate on the use of terms such as "Islamist" and "fundamentalism". There are two issues in particular that ought to be addressed. The first relates to Haideh Moghissi's discussion of the term fundamentalist.

Moghissi suggests that although the term fundamentalist originated in the West in reference to Protestantism, it remains useful in describing particular Islamic movements. She writes,

> To distance themselves from stereotypical analyses, authors use the term fundamentalism reluctantly and apologetically to describe new radical Islamic movements. Otherwise they offer substitute terms for it such as "revivalist," "religious nationalists," "Islamic radicals," "Islamic populists" or "Islamists" (2002, p. 65).

For Moghissi, the terms "Islamism" and "Islamists" can refer to three groups of people. The first are apolitical individuals or groups whose main concerns are religious (ibid., pp. 66–67). The second group consists of "Islamic liberal reformers" who "try to reform their societies according to the precepts of Islam, and at the same time to adjust Islam to the needs of modern times" (ibid., p. 67).

The third group covers the "fundamentalists". This group emerged in response to the "humiliations experienced by Middle Eastern societies under imperialist domination and later superpower rivalries" (ibid.). One feature of fundamentalist ideology is the concept of a past golden age which can be regained through a return to the text or past models such as Medina. The perceived degeneracy of contemporary Islamic societies is seen to be owing to deviations from true Islam (ibid., p. 69). Fundamentalists reject the separation of politics and religion, and in more democratic countries they seek to form government (ibid., p. 70). However, despite the sometimes democratic means by which fundamentalists attempt to form government, Moghissi describes them as "anti-democratic by virtue of their exclusionary stance" because "[t]heir attention is focused on the Muslim *umma*" (ibid., p. 71).

I should note that in her book, *Feminism and Islamic Fundamentalism*, Moghissi barely makes mention of Southeast Asia. Malaysia's ethnic composition, of which Muslims make up somewhat more than half, means that the divide between Islamists/fundamentalists and progressives/liberals consequently results in a different dynamic compared to those countries in the Middle East that have overwhelming Muslim majorities. For me "Islamist" seems the best word to describe those who wish to Islamize the social, political, and legal life of Malaysia. I might also add that the term fundamentalist does not adequately catch the Islamizing initiatives of UMNO, the goal of which is to infuse Islam into Malaysian law and politics through a process of guided evolution rather than through revolution (see Chapter 3).

A second issue in using terms such as Islamization, Islamist, and fundamentalism refers to the implication that the characteristics referred to become those that are definitively Islamic. The perceived essence of any religious or otherwise ideological movement is seldom if ever without significant variation and contest among those who identify with it. By our referring to them as Islamists and fundamentalists, those who we might also call traditionalists or conservatives seem to be ascribed with the default or most essential figuration of what Islam is. But there is no entirely satisfactory way out of this quandary (see also Martinez 2005, p. 136). I will use the word "Islamist" to refer to those people who advocate instilling or creating that which, in their view, is Islamic or in accord with the demands of orthodox Islam. "Islamization" refers in this book then to the process of instilling and creating that which is in ostensible accord with orthodox conservative Islam.

ISLAM AND REPRESSION

The treaties made between the British and the Sultans during Malaysia's colonial period removed the Sultans' powers in all areas except "Malay Religion and Custom". The formerly powerful Sultans of the different Malay states thus retained efficacy in just one realm, that of *adat* (Malay custom) and Islam. William R. Roff observes that

> [t]he rulers and traditional elite, much of whose real power to influence the destiny of their states had been stripped from them by the circumstances of British rule, not unnaturally turned to the only fields now left to them, religion and custom, to express what remained (1967, p. 72).

Thus we can see the importance that would have come to be placed on Islam as both a marker of Malay identity and as an area of political

autonomy. As well as "responding to a real need", notes Roff, the legal and
bureaucratic development of Islam may be "seen as a reflection of the desire
to emulate Western administrative systems in a field the Malays felt to be
peculiarly their own" (ibid.).

Referring to more recent developments, Syed Ahmad Hussein has noted
that the constriction of democratic spaces that occurred under Mahathir —
achieved using the rhetoric of a need for strong government — necessitated
the use of other spaces by those who, for various reasons, were unhappy
with political developments or had not benefited from Malaysia's economic
success (2002, p. 89). For many Malays in Malaysia, this was Islam, which
expanded to enable political criticisms. Syed writes that

> the tightening of the political arena had helped steer Islamists into new
> areas of dissent — that of social justice, clean government, democratic
> space, honest elections, rights and freedoms. To them, these were as central
> to the teachings of Islam as the Islamic programmes and institutions that
> UMNO had initiated (ibid.).

A few scholars have suggested that Islamism is a response to the failure
of secular mechanisms to enable redress for social and political grievances,
and of secular nation-states to deliver promised economic benefits. William
F. S. Miles argues that the failure of nationalism to unite disparate cultures
and ethnicities and to advance economic development has, in the face of
unequal distribution of benefits and concomitant popular aggrievement,
left "people yearning for alternative systems of hope" (1996, p. 531). Miles
goes on to say that where this occurs, those politicians who are willing to
use religious discourses for political gain — he calls them para-theologians
— step in to fulfil this need (ibid.).

Indeed, by the early 1970s in the Muslim world, according to Robert
W. Hefner, "the secular, socialist, and nationalist stars that had once shone
so brightly had begun to lose their luster" (2005, p. 19; see also Geertz
1973, p. 235). The need for an ethical compass led to a popular civil
resurgence in Islam (Hefner 2005, p. 20) and, "[i]n light of its scale and
the competition among its promoters, it was inevitable that at some point
religious entrepreneurs would move to channel the resurgence's social capital
into political ends" (ibid., p. 21). The political use to which Islam was put,
Hefner goes on to note, was made all the more likely as "religious associations were among the few public arenas in which ordinary people could
make their voices heard" (ibid.; see also Langman 2005, p. 263; Dorraj
1999, p. 228; Gilsenan 2000, pp. 43–44; Hibbard and Little 1997, p. 42;
Watson 2000, p. 207).

The appeal to religion to play a political role (when other means have been greatly constrained or closed) predictably leads to the articulation of a politico-religious framework in which the political and religious realms are construed as inseparable. That the religious and political realms are inseparable is a claim frequently made of Islam and indeed the conditions in which Islam emerged encouraged a close association between Islam and political management. Dominique Colas writes that

> [w]hereas Christianity developed on the periphery of the Roman Empire and little by little conquered the centre ... the political construction of the state in the Middle East and North Africa followed a model of conquest involving the importation of a faith, a language — Arabic — and organization into caliphates. ... It is not then Islam itself but the conditions of its expansion that explain the absence of differentiation between civil society and the state (1997, pp. 97–98; see also Armstrong 1993, p. 165).

A useful illustration of religion being brought into a political register according to need is Christian liberation theology. Liberation theology developed, among other things, to mobilize the public to protest against social injustices (Dorraj 1999, p. 230). According to Manochehr Dorraj, "[l]iberation theologians negated the avowed separation of state and church as the invention of 'the bourgeois church,' and cited the example of Jesus who suffered and fought against the social injustice of his day" (ibid.).

Jean-Pierre Reed and John Foran (2002) have explored how, in Nicaragua, arbitrary State repression and the lack of formal channels for dispute or redress led to the emergence in the 1970s of two frameworks which assimilated the experiences and feelings of disaffection and provided avenues for action. These were Catholic liberation theology and Sandinismo, of which I shall only discuss the former.

Reed and Foran note that "religious expressions of political opposition came out of a pre-existing popular idiom" (ibid., p. 345). They give examples of the justifications of people who took up arms against the government. One of these was a peasant who said, "I used to take [courses] on religious matters and ... we used to reflect on how Christ wanted the poor to live, on how Christ wanted people to live, on the rights of the person, on equality. ... These things led us to believe that the only alternative was to overthrow the government" (ibid.). A second man, a Spanish missionary who, after finding no success in improving the lot of the peasants with whom he worked, "came to believe that the only recourse to better the lot of Nicaragua's peasantry and poor was to take up arms as a Christian militant" (ibid., p. 347).

Reed and Foran regard the framework of liberation theology as a "political culture of opposition". Referring to examples such as those I cited above, they write that

> [t]hese retrospective accounts suggest that the ideology embodied in liberation theology, as constructed at a series of high-level Church conferences in the 1960s and 1970s, encountered a pre-existing cultural reality, a currency of Christian idioms, in Nicaragua. Familiarity with Christian homilies and the wide currency of popular religious principles in Nicaraguan society contributed to the articulation of new and radical claims within the context of changing political realities. The resulting amalgam, which we see as the *political culture* of liberation theology, allowed Nicaraguans to make sense of the experiences of political repression and social inequality by giving fresh politicized connotations to long-standing notions of "salvation" and "sin," and coupling them with familiar but newly signified terms such as "exploitation," "the place of the poor," "the rights of the person," "equality," "justice," and "liberation," among others (ibid., p. 351; emphasis original).

The development of a theologically founded militancy has also been described by James Toth in Egypt. He notes that in the context of economic disorder in the 1990s, some of Egypt's public sought non-government avenues when they could not influence the government legitimately. As the secular left had been marginalized, "guidance came from middle-class radicals who joined the Islamist movement and who galvanized mass discontent into a serious challenge to the state" (2005, p. 120).

In the same way that discontent in Nicaragua became articulated through pre-existing Christian idioms, so too in Egypt did the same occur in the Islamic idiom. The Muslim profession of faith, the *shahada*, played such a role. Toth notes that the *shahada*, which states that, "There is no god but God, and Muhammad is His Messenger", presented "a program for revolutionary action in today's modern world: reject as polytheism all authority that is elevated to the level of God, and reject as unbelief all codes but those contained in the Qur'an" (ibid., p. 121).

Toth explores the context and history behind the growth of the Islamic movement in Egypt's southern region. That region, Sa'id, is less developed than the rest of Egypt and State budgets have neglected it (ibid., p. 123). White-collar professionals from there were discriminated against and were unable to follow the professional careers of other Egyptians. Consequently they "re-activated" the religious ideas they learnt at college and while working overseas in Libya, Iraq, and the Gulf. They went on to "emulate the Prophet Muhammad, to grow beards and dress in white robes, and to perform charitable acts and good deeds that would bring them closer to their religion" (ibid., p. 124). As a result, they won allegiance from those they helped and "when the burning question turned to radically refashioning what many saw as a profoundly corrupt and dishonest government, the fundamental reply simply became 'Islam'" (ibid., p. 128). Toth goes on to note that

> [w]hile many still remained hopeful that the political and election process would eventually establish a legitimate avenue for social change, a growing number moved beyond the limits of peaceful transformation as they began to realize that militancy offered the only practical way to fundamentally change state and society (ibid., p. 130).

Whatever its origins, the existence of religious militancy can legitimize further repression instead of forcing a regime to change its approach. The threat of extremism or terrorism can be used to justify a state of emergency and so enable the State to act with impunity. Following 11 September 2001, several people were detained in Malaysia under the ISA for allegedly belonging to the terrorist organization Kumpulan Militan Malaysia (KMM, or Malaysian Militant Group) and for planning terrorist acts. Among them was Nik Adli Nik Aziz, who is the son of the spiritual leader of PAS, Nik Aziz Nik Mat (Noor 2003, p. 223). The lawyer for some of the accused, Edmund Bon, related to me that the KMM label was used to plant fear into the population. KMM was initially announced by the police as standing for Kumpulan Mujahidin Malaysia. Mujahidin refers to freedom fighters and was used positively to refer to the jihadi resistance to Soviet occupation in Afghanistan. Changing "Mujahidin" to "Militan" made the group more threatening and distanced it from a cause to which many were sympathetic.

News reports of what was seized in connection to the arrests included, among other things, a map of Port Klang. Reports implied that one of Malaysia's main ports was a target of KMM's planned terrorist activities (see, for example, Marhalim 2002). However, at no time during the questioning of the arrestees, Bon informed me, were they asked about these maps or about a plot to target that port. This indicated to him that the exercise served, minimally, to frighten the public with the spectre of Islamic terrorism.

Invented or otherwise, KMM's purported existence helps to scare the general public into accepting the necessity of such mechanisms as the ISA and for authoritarianism in general. This may hold true in Egypt too. Holger Albrecht writes with regard to the Muslim Brotherhood, which is Islamist but not militant, that "[i]t is rational for the regime to grant the Muslim Brotherhood some public space in order to uphold the fears of the 'Islamist threat,' by which coercive measures can be legitimized and thereby prolong the state of emergency and control elections" (2005, p. 390).

REPRESSION AND RESISTANCE

Expressions of disaffection need not be as open as participation in opposition parties, NGOs, or militant groups. James C. Scott pioneered the anthropological enquiry into what he calls "everyday forms of resistance". Focusing on peasants, he defines such resistance as, "any act by a peasant (or peasants) that is intended either to mitigate or deny claims ... made of that class by superordinate classes ... or to advance peasant claims ... vis-à-vis these superordinate classes" (Scott 1987, p. 419; see also Scott 1985, p. 290; some parentheses omitted). Examples of such resistance include foot-dragging, slander, arson, and sabotage (1987, p. 419). According to Scott they have the virtue of requiring "little or no planning, they often represent forms of individual self-help, and they typically avoid any direct symbolic confrontation with authority or with elite norms" (ibid., pp. 419–20).

Scott suggests that along a continuum of resistance from petty individual acts to durable movements of broad ideological purpose, the latter forms of resistance would form but "a very small, if vital, sector of that continuum" (Scott 1987, p. 419). Indeed, he suggests that everyday resistance is "often the most significant and the most effective over the long run" (1985, p. xvi). I would not suppose, however, that everyday forms of resistance are capable of addressing all forms of repression. Scott himself notes that "[t]he parameters of resistance are also set, in part, by the institutions of repression" (ibid., p. 299).

Repression comes in many forms. "Structural violence", writes Paul Farmer, is "exerted systematically — that is indirectly — by everyone who belongs to a certain social order" (2004, p. 307). Importantly, it is "structured and *stricturing*. It constricts the agency of its victims" (ibid., p. 315; emphasis original). This constriction of people's agency reduces their capacity to act in resistance, especially when people are as powerless as many of the Guatemalan poor about whom Farmer writes.

Similar to Farmer's structural violence is the mode of power Eric Wolf referred to as "structural power". "Structural power shapes the social field of action so as to render some kinds of behaviour possible, while making others less possible or impossible" (Wolf 2002, p. 223). It "organizes and orchestrates", Wolf writes, "the settings themselves and that specifies the distribution and direction of energy flows" (ibid.). To the distribution and direction of energy flows I might add that structural power could also include the presence of a moral cosmology which casts certain behaviours as immoral and hence punishable. The moral cosmology in turn describes the place of categories of person within that order — whether integral or peripheral — and consequently affects the distribution and direction of energy and different forms of capital.

It is thus important for those categories of people who are systematically discriminated against or taken advantage of to challenge the system that enables the abuse. For example, Teh Yik Koon has described how, when transsexual Malaysians have been caught by either police or religious authorities, they experience numerous abuses including being asked to display their breasts and genitals and being "invited" to have sex (Teh 2001). Ending such abuse requires that the indecency and other laws with which transsexuals are apprehended be amended and the (frequently Islamic) discourses that describe transexualism as indecent and deviant be challenged.

Thus, when discrimination is systematic, the form of resistance needs to target the framework that enables that system. In the Malaysian case, as I will later show, there are categories of person who suffer because of legal structures that authorize punitive measures against them. Perhaps the most important of these political and legal frameworks in contemporary Malaysia is that of Islam. Its cosmology, as it is manifest in Malaysia, gives precedence to Muslims over non-Muslims, and then to Sunni Muslims before others, and within that to those who follow the Shafi'i school, and males before females. And given that much of the evident push that Islam is receiving is State endorsed, the concerns and dissatisfactions of those who stand to lose come to be directed at the State. Others whose concerns relate to ostensibly non-ethnic and non-religious issues, such as the welfare of so-called "illegal" workers, also find that the State's laws and apparatuses play important roles in various deplorable practices. This especially applies to those wishing to repeal draconian legislation and to encourage a more liberal and less authoritarian government in Malaysia.

DEMOCRACY AND ACTIVISM

Speaking of the relationship between activism and the *sine qua non* of democracy, elections, William Case argues that in Southeast Asia, transitions from semidemocracy (which he describes Malaysia as being) to fuller democracy have not been brought about by the actions of voters acting only as voters. Voters at best "only initiate the transformative blow, rather than seeing it through" (2005, p. 227). Instead transition has only occurred "where they have grown so agitated by the government's distorting their electoral preferences they have turned finally to popular upsurge" (ibid., p. 225).

A precondition for popular dissatisfaction with ruling regimes is declining economic prosperity. When the economy slows or retreats, "inversely varying fortunes between elites and mass publics" result in social grievances intensifying (ibid., p. 224). When economic conditions deteriorate, according to Case, governments can respond artfully or otherwise. An example of an artful response was that of the Singaporean government during the 1997–98 economic crisis. Singaporeans faced economic hardships and the government lowered wages and contributed less to superannuation. "However, the government also reduced the salaries of its ministers — a measure unveiled with much fanfare — shrewdly avoiding societal grievances over inverse distributions. And it pledged to restore citizens' retirement benefits as soon as the economy had recovered" (ibid., p. 228). This largely symbolic sharing of the burden helped to diffuse popular resentment.

The Malaysian government, on the other hand, did not act as artfully during the same period. The government bailed out large well-connected companies by drawing on funds from its national superannuation scheme. Consequently, "the fortunes of favored elites and hard-pressed mass publics varied inversely, catalysing societal grievances into demands for political reform" (ibid., p. 229). But the Malaysian government was not completely unartful. It also portrayed the opposition parties as economically incompetent, as violent, and besmirched the reputation of Anwar Ibrahim who had embodied victimization by a corrupt government. Thus the government managed to win 55 per cent of the popular vote in 1999 and retained its two-thirds majority of seats in Parliament.

Because the response of the Malaysian government was not wholly unartful, popular upsurge was less overpowering compared to where governments were less able to manage popular sentiment. According to Case, the Philippines, Indonesia, and Myanmar were examples of the latter. In Indonesia and the Philippines the popular upsurges led to greater democratization. In Myanmar it led to hard military authoritarianism (ibid., pp. 231, 234).

Valerie Bunce similarly argues that the most successful democratic transitions in post-communist Eastern European countries began with mass protests (2003, p. 172). These protests "signalled the breakdown of the authoritarian order", "created a widespread sense that there were alternatives to that order" and created "a large opposition united by its rejection of the incumbent regime" (ibid.).

A situation such as this in Malaysia was perhaps most apparent in recent times in the form of a series of rallies in Kuala Lumpur prior to the

2008 elections, all seeking redress from one or another State institution. Well before these rallies, however, Meredith Weiss and Saliha Hassan had noted that activism in Malaysia tends to be directed towards the State (2004, p. 9). They also note that many NGOs and opposition parties share common impediments, "such as the narrow space and limited freedom allowed for alternative political discourses and activism, the need for greater consideration for human rights, and the significance of promoting a viable civil society to further Malaysia's political developments" (ibid., p. 11). Owing to the similar refrains coming from both these quarters, the Malaysian government tends to consider them both as aligned (ibid.). Ooi Kee Beng writes that "the boundary between non-government organizations and opposition parties with regards to both personnel and issues, tends to be indistinct" (in Ooi, Saravanamuttu, and Lee 2008, p. 10).

Part of the reason that civil society and opposition parties share a good deal of common ground is that the BN coalition repeatedly affirms that its use of repressive mechanisms, such as the ISA, is legitimized by its consistent electoral victories. UMNO parliamentarian Mohamed Nazri Aziz argued at a public debate on the ISA held in the Selangor Chinese Assembly Hall in 2005, that the BN's electoral victories indicate approval by Malaysians of the laws that activists decry. According to Nazri, "[i]f the voters pick a Barisan government, it means they want the ISA and if they choose the opposition, they do not want the ISA" (Edwards 2004).

Indeed, electoral success is used to legitimize all and sundry of the government's policies. It is thus an important legitimacy for activists and opposition party politicians to challenge. Likewise is the government's two-thirds parliamentary majority; this majority has enabled the BN to make and amend laws, including the Constitution, at will. This two-thirds majority has been regarded as particularly important to erode as it would prevent the BN unilaterally making and amending laws that hobble the opposition and many civil society activities.

The relationship between NGOs, activists, and opposition parties that flowered during a peak in popular discontent around the time of the Asian financial crisis in the late 1990s is understandable when it is realized that the BN is the common source of the erosion of civil liberties, government transparency, and the independence of the judiciary. Graham K. Brown notes that the formation of the Barisan Alternatif (Alternative Front) coalition, which was in official effect during the 1999 and 2004 elections, is an example of the coming together of opposition parties and civil society. The Barisan Alternatif consisted of PKR, the Democratic Action Party (DAP), and PAS, and was formed in 1999 as a result of the momentum of "societal coalitions, involving both civil society and opposition groups" (2004, p. 106). There were various developments during Mahathir Mohamad's Prime Ministership that expanded the common ground of these groups. These were "most notably the centralization of power in the executive, the undermining of judicial independence, the exponential increase in money politics and its associated corruption, and the abuse of basic freedoms" (ibid., p. 105).

While Ooi suggests that opposition parties and civil society actors intentionally blur the distinction between these groups (in Ooi, Saravanamuttu, and Lee 2008, p. 10), I think that more often opposition parties and NGOs have an ambivalent relationship. Although they share grievances with regard to the legal and political frameworks that hinder their ability to function, many non-party-affiliated people see association with opposition political parties as detrimental to themselves and the potential success of the agendas they wish to promote. As a result, NGO campaigns may even shun support from opposition parties on the grounds that they wish not to make their campaign "political", or for it to be politically "neutral".

The desire for given campaigns, movements, and bodies to have no association with opposition political parties is an understandable frustration to the latter. In 2001, for instance, Sivarasa Rasiah was barred from being a member of the Malaysian Bar Council[1] upon being appointed to the post of vice-president of PKR. This was owing to section 46 of the Legal Professions Act which forbids members of the Bar Council from holding office in a political party or trade union. Although a court challenge failed to have section 46 declared unconstitutional, what was troubling for Sivarasa was that the majority of members of the Bar Council supported the court's decision and, furthermore, they sought and found other "technical grounds" to support Sivarasa's expulsion from the committee. As Latheefa Koya, a PKR member, lawyer, and activist, wrote in response,

> In its desperate attempt to look "independent," the Bar Council has decided to take a "neutral" stand regarding issues of fundamental rights and liberties. With cries of democracy, liberty and justice being suppressed further, one cannot remain neutral. How can one not take a stand? So what if the stand happens to be similar to opposition voices; especially when it comes to issues which deal with fundamental rights and liberties? (Latheefa 2001).

The commonly expressed wish of bodies or campaigns to remain politically "neutral" is usually a euphemistic way of expressing a desire not to be associated with opposition parties. Given that the condition of the law and status quo is usually biased in favour of the BN, the effect of this neutral stand is to entrench further the coalition which has ruled since Malaysia's independence in 1957. This stand is taken because groups fear that their agendas will be rejected by the government by the mere presence of this association and that retributions may follow (see Scott 1985, pp. 274–81, for realizations of these fears in the village in which he worked in northern Malaysia). Iris Marion Young points out that in the realm of the political, the promotion and exchange of views for deliberation is not the mutually edifying enterprise as it is sometimes portrayed. It is agonistic. "Deliberation is competition. Parties to dispute aim to win the argument, not achieve mutual understanding" (1996, p. 123). The presence then of an opposition party could hinder a campaign as the campaign's success may be interpreted as the incumbent administration's loss. Parties, groups, and individuals who face essentially the same fundamental set of impediments, such as the constricting of their democratic space and the unaccountability of a regime, can thus find themselves working at cross purposes and even to their mutual disadvantage.

In April 2005, for instance, the youth wing of PAS called for the de-registering and the banning of the NGO, Sisters in Islam (SIS). This followed SIS's support for a campaign to end moral policing following the raid of a nightclub in Kuala Lumpur by the Federal Territory Islamic Department (described in Chapter 7). PAS regarded this campaign and SIS's support for it as contrary to the teachings of Islam. But in an article titled, "PAS 'hypocritical' in demanding ban on SIS", independent news website *Malaysiakini.com* reported that "[w]hen the rights of PAS were being violated by the ruling government over the past few years, human rights groups [including SIS] — whether they agreed with the Islamic party's policies — came to the defence of the opposition group" (Malaysiakini.com 2005*a*). Quoting a press statement by human rights NGO, Suara Rakyat Malaysia (the People's Voice of Malaysia), the article went on to report that "[t]he attempts by PAS to silence groups and individuals who hold different views and opinions is highly perplexing, given that PAS is not unfamiliar with the undemocratic and destructive nature of the suppression of the freedom to express."

THE ROLE OF THE VANGUARDS

Robert W. Hefner has examined the role of civic associations in the creation of democracy and has noted that, "nary a word is said about how civic associations may be cross-cut by deep ethnic, religious, or ideological divides" which, "rather than serving as social capital for democracy, at times these divisions can engender debilitating social rivalries that diminish rather than enhance the prospects for civic decency" (2001, p. 9). He notes that the plural societies of Southeast Asia are prime candidates for ethnic and religious divisions to endanger democracy and civil society. Hefner's point is demonstrated here by the example of the exclusionary stance of the youth wing of PAS, whose own democratic space has in the past been constricted by the government.

Hefner is not the first to point out how mutually disadvantaged groups can work against improving or challenging the system which represses or exploits them. Maurice Merleau-Ponty, in citing Vladimir Lenin, points out that the interests of the proletariat would have been better served if not for the proletariat's many divisions. These divisions include, among other things, those according to territory, trade, and religion (Merleau-Ponty 1969, p. 117). These divisions prevent them from apprehending their fundamental common identity as the working class and, thus, prevent them from taking effective action to improve their political position.

Parallels are to be found in Malaysia. Groups or categories of people may have multiple identities of which the most salient and most affective may, however, dispose different groups to mobilize against each other rather than a more fundamental common source of repression. The phrase "divide and rule" is commonly used to refer to elite management of Malaysian society and politics. It initially described British colonial policy in which the different ethnicities were kept separate in order to prevent their coalition and also to focus their fears and frustrations at each other rather than at the British (Abraham 2005, p. xviii; see also Singh 2001). Now it is used to describe BN coalition tactics of maintaining an undercurrent of hostility between the major ethnicities such that they come to depend on the BN for social stability.

However, Karl Marx himself suggested that "[t]he first phase in the struggle of the proletariat against the bourgeoisie is marked by sectarian movements. These are justified in an age when the proletariat is not yet developed enough to act as a class" (Marx 1971). To advance the proletariat beyond sectarian movements, what is needed, according to Merleau-Ponty, is "a Party which clarifies the proletariat to itself" (1969, p. 117). The Party must connect the particular situation of the proletariat to the wider scheme. Echoing Lenin's point, he writes, "Local history must have a patent connection with universal history without which the proletariat lapses into the provincialism it should have transcended" (ibid., p. 119). That is, the Party must help the proletariat transcend the potentially obscuring specificities of their circumstance to see themselves in the wider scheme, as subject to a more general system of exploitation which must be overthrown. As David Lane put it, socialist intellectuals, from Lenin's perspective, "play an important role in bringing 'theory' to manual workers: ideas which explain their social position and their role in history to them" (1981, p. 46).

When Marx speaks of the Party, he (at least sometimes) does so abstractly, "in the great historical sense of the word" (McLellan 1971, p. 174). It should be clear that in terms of their respective situations, there are correlations between the Party and activists, the proletariat and society generally, and communism and democracy. Advocates or vanguards attempt to conscientize the exploited or repressed groups by informing them of the "reality" of their position and of their place in a wider picture. The solution proffered for their upliftment is the attainment and practice of a particular social and political system.

However, merely informing or demonstrating to people of a particular category that they are repressed or exploited does not mean that they will act to reform, challenge, or overthrow the system that exploits them. Jean-Paul Sartre notes that while communist revolutionaries can only be found among the oppressed,

> it does not suffice to be oppressed to choose to be a revolutionary. The Jews can be classed with the oppressed — and the same holds true for racial minorities in certain countries — but many of them are oppressed within the bourgeoisie and, as they share the privileges of the class which oppresses them, they are unable, without contradiction, to work for the destruction of these privileges (1955, p. 209).

The task of untangling ethnicity, religion, class, or any identity thread from others is a difficult task. Life is necessarily permeated with ambivalence. Furthermore, as Cornelius Castoriadis opines, "in my view it appears more than superficial to present [ethnic conflict and racism] ... as something wholly fabricated by classes or by political groups for the purpose of assuring or achieving their position of dominance" (1997*a*, p. 26). Psychologists have long known the ease with which a strong sense of group-membership can be formed among even arbitrarily composed groups (Boyer 2002, p. 329; Tajfel 1970).

To be socially effective, however, discourses rely on extant themes in the society in question (Jackson 1983, especially p. 131). For the civil society activist, the politician, and the Marxist revolutionary alike, the discourses they deploy to advance their agenda must resonate with their audiences. The manner in which Marxists understand a society may appear to them to be true. But however true it might be, articulating it to the working-class in Marxist terms may not be effective. As Merleau-Ponty writes, "Class consciousness is not an absolute knowledge of which the proletarians are miraculously the trustees. It has to be formed and straightened out, but the only valid politics is the one which makes itself accepted by the workers" (1974, p. 51).

Even if one's espoused worldview catches on and leads to social change, if not revolution, that does not mean that the action taken to overcome repression might not engender its own set of repressive discourses, apparatuses, or mechanisms. Lila Abu-Lughod makes this point with regard to the resistance of young Bedouin women against restrictions enforced by their elders. A conflict that Abu-Lughod explores is the "deceptively frivolous issue" of lingerie and other feminine adornments. Insistence on having such products in the face of the older generation's protests constitutes younger women's resistance to older forms of family based authority (1990, p. 50). However, "[i]n resisting the axes of kin and gender, the young women who want lingerie ... are perhaps unwittingly enmeshing themselves in an extraordinarily complex set of new power relations" (ibid., pp. 51–52). These power relations relate to the Egyptian economy and to the State, "many of whose powers depend on separating kin groups and regulating individuals" (ibid.). By rejecting kin-based authority and aiming for a more secluded, sedentary, and typically Egyptian (as opposed to Bedouin) lifestyle, the young women become dependent on the favours of their husbands for what they want. Whereas Bedouin women had relied on their kinsmen to ensure good treatment from their husbands, this new situation disables that and enables husbands to punish and reward their wives by controlling their wives' access to their wants (ibid., pp. 49, 50).

Abu-Lughod points out that "[i]f the systems of power are multiple, then resisting at one level may catch people up at other levels" (ibid., p. 53). In the same way, groups that disavow support from opposition political parties in Malaysia reinforce the larger undemocratic framework which may ultimately be responsible for the problem which the group is trying to ameliorate. In the case of political Islam, if Islamism is a reaction to an unresponsive, corrupt, and unaccountable government, then the utilization and consequent legitimization of an Islamic discourse may often carry with it other sets of power relations and injustices. These include a de facto clergy that holds itself as unquestionable, construals of Syariah law that disfavour women, and an Islamic state that marginalizes non-Muslims.

A resistance discourse can also be co-opted by a ruling regime. Karen Armstrong notes with regard to the Syariah movement in history, that, "[l]ike all Islamic piety, the Shariah was also political. It constituted a protest against a society that was deemed by the religious to be corrupt" (2002, p. 61). The Syariah movement had an egalitarian ethos and sought to restrict the power of the caliph who had been raised to the Prophet's level of sanctity (ibid.).

However, discourses or ideologies that were founded in response or in protest to a given situation can develop a functional autonomy from those roots. The functional autonomy of discourses and ideologies[2] allows them (and their legitimacy) to be co-opted by that at which they were aimed.

> The Shariah began as a protest movement, and much of its dynamism derived from its oppositional stance. Under the Ottoman system, this was inevitably lost. The *ulama* became dependent upon the state. As government officials, the sultan and his *pashas* could — and did — control them by threatening to withdraw their subsidies. Abu al-Sund Khola Chelebi (1490–1574), who worked out the principles of the Ottoman-*ulama* alliance, made it clear that the *qadis* (judges) derived their autonomy from the sultan, the guardian of the Shariah, and were therefore bound to apply the law according to his directives. Thus the Shariah was made to endorse the system of absolute monarchy (now more powerful than ever before) which it had been originally designed to oppose (Armstrong 2002, pp. 133–34).

The Syariah movement and the Islamist discourse in Malaysia appear to share similar fates. Syed Husin Ali writes that

> [t]he religious functionaries from the mufti and the kadi right down to the imam, bilal and noja are holders of positions that have been bureaucratised. They have become government servants who are paid monthly salaries, appointed on the basis of selection and merit, and can be promoted or demoted, depending on circumstances. It is not surprising, therefore, that some of them have become mere tools of the government in the name of religion ... (2008a, p. 67).

Thus, in the name of religion, one set of repressions can be overlaid on a prior set, resulting in a more restrictive and repressive condition. Islam comes to be politicized and politics comes to be Islamized. Thus credit is given to Sartre's observation that "to fight something one must change oneself into it" (1969, p. 63), and Hegel's assertion that when "religious principles come into play, the only possible course is for the government to resort to force and suppress the opposing religion or treat its adherents as a [political] party" (1999, p. 231; parentheses original).

Resistance and opposition to repression can, as noted earlier, possibly exacerbate authoritarianism. First, as in the case of Islamic extremism, it can provide an ostensible threat to the social order and so legitimize coercive repression. Second, as in the case of opposition parties contesting unfair elections, it can portray a regime as legitimately elected. And third, oppositional discourses can be co-opted by the regime at which they were initially aimed and result in an even more repressive and complicated environment.

But at the same time, activists and activist groups do experience successes against repression and against the odds. There have been unlikely court successes by indigenous communities against the government. One of these was a compensation claim by the Temuan community of Kampung Bukit Tampoi, Selangor, against, *inter alia*, the state government of Selangor and the federal government who were alleged to have deprived the community of their land without compensation (see Nicolas 2005). Another example, though not quite so complete, is the result attained in the Court of Appeal in Ms Shamala Sathiyaseelan's custody case which I describe in Chapter 6.

Whether these advances outweigh the regressions, or whether they in fact merely serve to give resistance a false sense of efficacy, is difficult to categorically determine. But certainly important is the public space in which challenges can be mounted and discontent may be expressed. It may be the case that this public space is too constricted. Indeed, criticism and disagreement may be against the law, as is the case in relation to *fatwa*. Where there is utterly and desperately no room for protest, and no response to those grievances that are aired, violence may be the only resort. This might be the position of the Egyptians from Sa'id and the Christian militants mentioned earlier, for whom conventional non-violent methods of bringing about change were ineffective.

Taking democracy to refer to the ability of people to participate in public life, to argue their cases in the discourses that they select, and so influence those processes which affect their lives, I explore in this book the means by which some Malaysians have attempted to enlarge meaningful democracy in Malaysia. The discourses made use of in framing the projects they devise have contexts and histories. These contexts and histories are important to understand to appreciate better the situation of activists described herein. Thus, it is to a description of these contexts to which I now turn in the two chapters that follow. In Chapter 2, I give a short pertinent history of Malaysia. In Chapter 3, I describe the debate over whether Malaysia is or ought to be an Islamic state.

Notes

1. The Malaysian Bar Council regulates the activities of the Malaysian Bar which "is an independent Bar whose aim is to uphold the rule of law and the cause of justice and protect the interest of the legal profession as well as that of the public. ... Each member advocate and solicitor is automatically a member of the Malaysian Bar so long as he/she holds a valid Practising Certificate" <http://www.malaysianbar.org.my/bar_council.html> (accessed 3 April 2009).
2. The notion of a functional autonomy of discourse has been adapted from the psychologist Gordon W. Allport's notion of a functional autonomy of motives (1937).

2

A SHORT HISTORY OF MALAYSIA

THE PRE-COLONIAL PERIOD

According to Alberto Gomes, archaeologists tend to agree that Malaysia's aboriginal populations are descendants of Neolithic and Hoabinhian humans who arrived more than 5,000 and 10,000 years ago respectively (1999, pp. 78–79). Those who are known today as Malays came later from what is now known as Indonesia.

West or peninsular Malaysia was in the path of a trade route between China and India. Sources indicate that Indian traders visited the peninsula in the first centuries C.E. The influence on Malay culture of these Indians persists in the form of language, political practices, art, and popular beliefs. Later, the peninsula lay in the path of trade between China, the Middle East, and the West (ibid., pp. 79–80).

In the 1400s a small settlement of Sumatran refugees became the trading centre for the region. Malacca, as it became known, was soon to host Malays, Arabs, Indians, Javanese, Sumatrans, Bugis, Borneons, Filipinos, Persians, and Chinese. Although these groups interacted with each other, they remained in their own ethnically polarized enclaves. In 1511 Malacca fell to the Portuguese. The Malay rulers and their subjects fled to other areas of the peninsula. Between 1500 and 1800 large numbers of Indonesian immigrants came to the various Malay states and displaced and even enslaved some of the indigenous people. In 1641 the Dutch took over

Malacca. Malacca was later taken over by the British in the 1800s along with the rest of peninsular Malaysia (ibid., p. 80).

THE BRITISH COLONIAL PERIOD

In the period between 1874 and the First World War, the British gained complete control of the Malay peninsula. The British found it difficult to induce Malays, who were largely agrarian, to work (Jomo 1990*a*, p. 4) and also felt that "the Malay, despite his charm, was indolent and shiftless and resistant to change and progress" (Roff 1967, p. 25). "Proletarianised immigrants" (Jomo 1990*a*, p. 4) from China and India were thus imported. Indentured Indian immigrants worked on rubber plantations, and many Chinese worked in tin mines.

Tin had been mined for centuries but was expanded by the British, especially in the state of Perak and particularly after the 1880s when railroads were installed. Chinese mine-operators rented land from Malay Sultans and large numbers of Chinese coolies were brought in to work in these mines. Under the British the Chinese dominated tin mining owing to their technology and organization until 1912, when direct political intervention and technological advances by the British allowed the latter to assert their own dominance.

As a result of colonial policies, the three main ethnicities of contemporary Malaysia were segmented occupationally and geographically. It should be pointed out that, as argued by Anthony Milner, the ethnic identities that have contemporary currency in Malaysia were not as apparent during colonial times. "[E]ven in the 1930s the terms 'Malay' and 'Chinese' still possessed a certain novelty in many quarters as social categories" and that before then Malays were likely to identify themselves according to the Sultan to whom they were subject or the locality from which they came (2003, p. 76). According to Milner, certain pre-colonial characteristics of Malay society served to keep differentiated the communities that came to be called the Malays and Chinese and that these groups came to have their contemporary ethnic identities by adopting colonial labelling conventions.

The Chinese and Indians were initially regarded as transient workers and a rise in homeland Chinese and Indian nationalisms led to strong identifications with their respective homelands rather than with Malaya, as Malaysia was known before 1963 (Funston 1980, p. 1). However, in 1931 a census of Malaya revealed that immigrants outnumbered Malays and that one-third of Chinese and one-quarter of Indians were locally born and showed trends of permanent settlement (Turnbull 1989, p. 200).

Malay objections to colonial immigration and labour policies then inten-
sified. The British attempted to pre-empt objections by affirming that
the immigrants were only transitory and by implementing "pro-Malay"
policies.

Chinese and Indians, however, had already been making demands and
by 1923, both had been conceded representation on the Straits Settlements
Legislative Council and on Malay State Councils. Owing to their homeland
loyalties the Chinese and Indians had not, however, been making demands
for citizenship. Meanwhile, and in spite of pro-Malay policies, Chinese made
gains in business, labour, and education and the Indians made headway in
the public and private sectors (Cheah 1999, pp. 101–102).

THE JAPANESE OCCUPATION

During the Second World War, the British were defeated by the Japanese
who occupied Malaya until the war's end. While in control of Malaya, the
Japanese stirred anti-European sentiments and massacred and persecuted
Chinese who formed the Malayan People's Anti-Japanese Movement and
the Malayan Communist Party (MCP). The Japanese then formed para-
military units which were composed mainly of Malays to fight Chinese
resistance.

The Japanese Occupation had a significant effect on political developments in Malaya. The Malay peasantry became politicized and this disposed
them to mobilization after the war. It also gave the people of Malaya
strengthened confidence in their struggle against colonialism (Funston 1980,
p. 35). In the words of former Prime Minister Mahathir Mohamad,

> The initial Japanese defeat of the Europeans did, however ... have [a]
> psychological effect on many Asians. ... Before the war, when Malaya was
> under British rule, our entire world-view was that we had no capability
> to be independent ... and felt we had to accept their superiority. But
> the success of the Japanese invasion convinced us that there is nothing
> inherently superior in the Europeans. They could be defeated, they could
> be reduced to grovelling before an Asian race, the Japanese (Mahathir
> 1999, p. 16).

The Japanese, however, surrendered in 1945. The Malayan People's
Anti-Japanese Movement then established *de facto* control in many towns
and cities. Among their first concerns were reprisals against Japanese col-
laborators who were, for the most part, Malays (Esman 1994, p. 52; see
also Syed H. A. 2008*b*, pp. 64–76). Malays in turn, led by religious leaders,

retaliated, which gave Malay nationalism further impetus (Funston 1980, p. 36).

Owing to Chinese resistance to and Malay collaboration with the Japanese, British plans for a Malayan Union, which aimed at unifying the country under direct British rule, did not give political precedence to the Malays. It granted equal rights and opportunities to residents regardless of race or background (Esman 1994, p. 52). However, the Malay response to the prospect of economic and political domination by the Chinese and Indians under the Malayan Union plan "was as rapid and decisive as it was unexpected from a people reputed to be politically passive" (ibid., p. 53).

It is worth noting at this point that the strength of the Islamic idiom was relatively weak and ethnic idioms were more often used to mobilize Malays. "*Hidup Melayu!*" (Long live the Malays!) was a common slogan and one adopted by UMNO in this pre-independence period (Mutalib 1990, pp. 21–22). Indeed, Mutalib notes that conferences on Islam held during the Japanese Occupation largely turned on matters of Malay ethnicity rather than addressing issues facing all Muslims (ibid., p. 17). In this pre-independence period there was significant willingness of Malays "to defend their ethnic interests against other communities, even if Muslim" (ibid., p. 20). With regard to UMNO's political orientation, Mutalib observes,

> The party leadership pledged its commitment to pursue the goals of Malay ethnic nationalism, which meant essentially the educational, economic, social, cultural, and political upliftment and dominance of the Malay community in Malayan affairs. Although UMNO initially had an Ulama Section, the latter played a limited role in influencing the leadership towards any kind of Islamic aspirations (ibid., p. 22).[1]

The significant mobilization that this ethnic nationalism managed to arouse, and the lack of substantial counter-mobilization by Chinese and Indians, led to British capitulation over the Malayan Union plan. As a result of the strength of UMNO, the plans for a Malayan Union were replaced by plans for the Federation of Malaya. These plans placed Malays in a dominant political position and limited the citizenship rights for non-Malays (ibid., p. 53)

After the inauguration of the Federation of Malaya on 1 February 1948, the MCP staged an armed insurrection. The MCP's front organizations and trade unions, which had opposed the Federation, were being frustrated by the British. From this time until 1989 the MCP continued its insurrection (Cheah 2002, p. 22). This had a considerable impact on the way Malaysia would develop. Repressive emergency laws which were introduced by the British to contain the insurrection were bequeathed to the incoming government. These laws permitted the detention of persons on the grounds of their suspected communist inclinations. Their detention without trial was indefinite. It might be noted that current restrictions on media freedoms share the same history (ibid., p. 33).

1957 TO 1969

The political place of the Malays and the non-Malays was negotiated prior to independence in 1957 and the compromises struck by the alliance members for the ethnic populations they claimed to represent became known as The Bargain and later, the "social contract". The Bargain did not result in any kind of written document, but the result was that the Malays were granted political precedence in exchange for citizenship rights for Chinese and Indians. A number of other concessions made by the Malaysian Chinese Association (MCA), the Malayan Indian Congress (MIC), and UMNO were recognitions of "the special position of the Malays", "Malay as the national language", and "Islam as the religion of the country" (Cheah 2002, p. 37). However, according to Mavis Puthucheary, the original contents of The Bargain cannot be determined and reference to it has been subject to political abuse by UMNO, which has used it to legitimize the political pre-eminence of Malays and thus itself (Puthucheary 2008).

In August 1963 Malaysia was formed after Singapore, Sarawak, and Sabah joined with Malaya. After the formation of Malaysia, Lee Kuan Yew, the leader of Singapore's ruling People's Action Party (PAP), began challenging the terms of The Bargain. Lee campaigned for ethnic equality and for a "Malaysian Malaysia", rather than one in which Malays were accorded a special position. Singapore was subsequently expelled from Malaysia in August 1965, but not before arousing discontent among the Chinese.

THE 1969 GENERAL ELECTIONS AND
THE 13 MAY RACE RIOTS

In May 1969 communal riots took place in Malaysia. Faaland, Parkinson, and Saniman (1990) identify four points that are important in understanding the cause of these riots which occurred three days after the 10 May 1969 general elections. First, Gerakan (which later joined the Barisan Nasional or BN in 1974) and the post-expulsion incarnation of the PAP, the Democratic Action Party (DAP), both ostensibly multi-ethnic parties but both dominated by Chinese members, questioned the rights of Malays which were ostensibly agreed to in The Bargain. Second, the DAP continued the PAP's campaign for a "Malaysian Malaysia". Third, the citizenship rights which were granted to the Chinese and Indians had a significant impact on the 1969 elections in the form of increased support for non-Malay opposition parties. Fourth, the economic position of Malays had not improved as expected (ibid., p. 13). In fact, inequalities appear to have increased, although not so much between groups as within them (Jomo 1990*b*, p. 470).

According to a government report, on the eve of the election, ten thousand people attended a funeral procession through the streets of Kuala Lumpur for a Labour Party activist who was killed in a clash with police. The Chinese processionals chanted and sang incendiary slogans including, "The East is Red", as well as displaying portraits of Mao Tse-Tung. They also provoked Malay passers-by with shouts of "*Malai si*" and "*Hutang darah di bayar darah*" ("Death to Malays" and "Blood debts will be repaid with blood") (Funston 1980, pp. 208–209).

Malay concerns about falling politically as well as economically behind seemed to be borne out by the results of the 1969 elections. The results showed a significant swing to the DAP and Gerakan. The swing dispossessed the ruling coalition of its two-thirds majority. The DAP and Gerakan subsequently organized celebratory rallies on 11 and 12 May. These rallies were even more provocative than the election eve funeral procession (ibid., p. 209). In response, Harun bin Haji Idris, Selangor's Chief Minister called for a pro-government demonstration. At this rally, Malay politicians claimed that "Malay supremacy in government was being challenged by infidels and that they needed to teach the Chinese a lesson" (Munro-Kua 1996, p. 55). Immediately prior to the demonstration, rumours that Malays had been attacked by Chinese in another part of Selangor reached the assembled crowd. This news incited the UMNO demonstrators into taking punitive revenge (Funston 1980, p. 209; cf Kua 2008).

The official number of people killed in the riots is 178 (Cheah 2002, p. 106). Those who were present in Malaysia at the time, however, believe many more than this died. Because the non-Malay deaths on 13 May outnumber Malay deaths by six to one, some observers have concluded that the military and police actively sided with the Malay rioters. Funston offers another interpretation:

> Part of the explanation may lie in instances of passive bias on the part of the security forces — failure to shoot members of their own race breaking the curfew, rather than shooting law-abiding members of a different race. In this respect it should be noted that security forces were trained to

combat communists of Chinese origin and were thus psychologically ill-equipped to act against Malays (Funston 1980, p. 210).

After the riots, Malaysia's first Prime Minister, Tunku Abdul Rahman, made a television appearance. In it he declared a State of Emergency for Selangor and a curfew on Kuala Lumpur. Responsibility for the riots was initially placed on non-Malay opposition parties, but in a following television appearance, blame was placed on communists. He later expanded the State of Emergency to cover the whole nation and appointed Tun Abdul Razak to a newly formed National Operations Council. Abdul Rahman was ostensibly unable to take charge of this council owing to ill health (ibid., pp. 211–12).

THE INTRODUCTION OF
THE NEW ECONOMIC POLICY

Abdul Razak made a major national address one month after the riots and spoke of a "new realism". This was to manifest itself in the establishment of a national ideology, the *Rukun Negara* (National Principles), and by making the educational system more Malay-oriented. There was also a prohibition against raising "sensitive issues" — namely questioning the privileged position of Malays. Sanctions were also placed on actions that might inflame tensions. To this end 7,500 people were arrested in the weeks after 13 May, though by July, 6,500 of these had been released (ibid., p. 213).

Prior to the reconvening of Parliament in 1971, the government launched its New Economic Policy (NEP). The NEP's main objectives were to "eliminate the identification of race with economic function" and to eradicate poverty, regardless of race. As Malays tended to have weaker economic positions and since it was mainly agrarian Malays who lived in poverty, the overall goals of the NEP would mainly benefit Malays (see Jomo 1990*a*). The removal of the association of race and economic function translated in practice into increasing Malay participation in the economy. There was no attempt to increase non-Malay participation in government or in agriculture.

Abdul Razak died in 1976 and was succeeded by his brother-in-law Hussein Onn. Hussein Onn's administration (1976–81) was brief but was characterized by attritions of fundamental liberties, although some of these were revoked after protest (Cheah 2002, p. 161). One that was not, however, was that persons detained under the ISA may be deprived of legal representation and need not be brought before a magistrate within twenty-four hours of arrest (ibid., p. 161).

Also during Hussein Onn's administration there was an increase in Islamic militancy. Of note was a deadly attack on Hindu shrines by a Muslim group calling themselves The Army of Allah. Another incident involved a Muslim extremist group that engaged in a number of conflicts including an attack on a police station in the southern town of Batu Pahat (ibid., pp. 166-67).

Cheah Boon Kheng (2002, pp. 167–69) notes that these events were symptoms of a more general increase in interest in Islam that was fanned, in part, by the Islamic revolution in Iran in 1979 (see Noor 2003, p. 204). Malaysia's Islamic revival movement was known as *dakwah* (proselytizing). It resulted in the formation of a number of Islamic groups. This movement also affected the Islamic political party PAS, in that *ulama* (religious teachers or leaders) took power from ethnically oriented leaders (see Noor 2003, p. 203). The *dakwah* movement resulted in more Malays adopting Arabic dress with many females beginning to cover their heads and sometimes their faces.

After a convincing win in the 1978 general elections, Hussein Onn stepped down in 1981 and was succeeded by the first non-royal Prime Minister, Mahathir Mohamad. Mahathir would become Malaysia's longest serving Prime Minister as well as its most visionary and outspoken. The economic bases for Malaysian nation-building became most clearly articulated under Mahathir with ambitious goals including having Malaysia become a Newly Industrializing Country, a precursor to later attaining Developed Nation (or "First World") status by 2020. However, the period of Mahathir's administration was marked by increased authoritarianism. Perhaps the most significant incident which illustrates this was Operasi Lalang (Operation Weed) in 1987 when 107 activists and opposition party members were detained under the ISA for publicly protesting against government interventions in Chinese language education (see Lee 2008*a*).

In addition to the coercive measures described throughout this book, one ideological means by which the BN generally, and UMNO in particular, maintains its grip on power, is through its instrumental use of the memory of the 13 May riots. Thus, at this point it is worth considering the significant impact of the 13 May riots and how ethno-politics have evolved since.

FEARS OF ETHNIC VIOLENCE AND THE MEMORY OF 1969

Ooi, Saravanamuttu, and Lee regard 13 May as Malaysia's "greatest fixation" (2008, p. 2). They suggest that the discourse of sensitive issues spawned by it and the fear of its recurrence has stunted the country's maturity, constrained public space, and "increased media control and parliamentary passivity" (ibid., p. 3). Pro-Malay policies are often more and less explicitly justified on the grounds of quelling the sentiments that led to those riots.

A reason that continues to be proffered by both Malays and non-Malays for the continuation of privileges is that, if Malay benefits were removed, they would be unable to compete against members of other ethnicities (Fenton 2003, p. 139; cf Milner 2003, pp. 11–19). One commonly cited example is with regard to university placements. As one Malaysian lamented to me, "non-Malays with straight 'A's cannot get in [to local universities] whereas Malays with the poorest of marks do."

At the fifty-fifth UMNO General Assembly in 2004, Prime Minister Abdullah Badawi said that Malays must be able to face the challenges of the global environment. He went on to say that

> Umno has a duty to help the Malays become stronger, more able, confident and courageous. … But in undertaking all these efforts, Umno should also prepare the Malay mind to face the realities of this world … If we fail to hone the competitive skills of the race, we will eventually become a defeated race. Malays will always be looked down upon, always feel insecure and lack confidence and be seen as a burden by others. … (Abdullah 2004).

It is sometimes observed that Malay discourses exhibit an underlying if not overt sense of being under threat. Virginia Matheson Hooker, in an examination of Malay novels until 1980, discovered consistent warnings that the Malay race and homeland were under threat of being overwhelmed by foreign races and of being overtaken in the march towards modernity (2000).

In March 2005 UMNO launched a programme entitled "*Melayu Dalam Bahaya*" ("Malays in Danger"). The programme consisted of seminars and included postings on UMNO-affiliated websites that criticized Malays for their failings and implied that other races were taking advantage of them (Nurul 2005). Azwanddin Hamzah of PKR condemned the sentiments and said, "If there is a riot, don't blame the opposition" (ibid.).

What is telling in Azwanddin's statement is the association of opposition parties with riots which required no expounding upon by the journalist. There has thus evolved a complex of closely connected ideas in Malaysian ethno-political discourse: the threat to Malay precedence and security by a Chinese-dominated opposition has developed into a fear of political instability should the BN lose dominance to the opposition per se.

Indeed, the possibility of ethnic violence is sometimes less an implicit fear than it is an explicit threat. At the same UMNO General Assembly cited above, UMNO deputy chairperson Badruddin Amiruldin waved a book about the 1969 riots in the air and warned that any challenge to Malay privileges would be akin to stirring a hornet's nest.

> "Don't poke at this nest, for if it were disturbed, these hornets will strike and destroy the country," he said to a thunderous applause from delegates attending the party's 55th annual general assembly at the Putra World Trade Centre in Kuala Lumpur...

> "Fifty-eight years ago we had an agreement with the other races, in which we permitted them to '*menumpang*' (temporarily reside) on this land. In the Federal Constitution, our rights as a race have been enshrined.

> "Let no one from the other races ever question the rights of Malays on this land. Don't question the religion because this is my right on this land," said the fiery orator to another round of applause (Fauwaz 2004).

A common notion in Malaysia is that the various affirmative action policies for Malays have resulted in, as Prime Minister Abdullah Badawi put it, Malays becoming dependent on crutches. This is sometimes referred to as a "subsidy mentality". The implications are, as evident in Abdullah's address cited earlier, that Malays are unable to compete with non-Malays on a level playing field whether locally or internationally. There have been various well-publicized attempts by UMNO politicians to craft positive identities for Malays to strive towards. These include the "New Malay" (Mahathir), the "Towering Malay" (Abdullah) and the "Glocal Malay" (Najib Tun Razak). These formulations usually emphasize economic competitiveness and Islamic piety. But as models to strive towards, they imply characteristics that Malays are supposed to currently lack: inspiring heights of excellence (Towering Malay), or bravery with a global outlook (Glocal Malay).

A consequence of the foregoing is that there is a confluence in the national imagination of, on the one hand, Malay entitlement to political pre-eminence and, on the other hand, insecurity over the ability of Malays to retain this position on merit owing to their ostensible non-competitiveness. In the near background, however, is the notion that Malay integrity can and will be secured through violence. The idea that ethnic Malays may, when they feel cheated, persecuted, or threatened, quickly turn to physical violence or rioting, entered the national consciousness with episodes such as the Maria Hertogh affair (see Chapter 5), but most importantly in 1969. The capacity for violence of the kind seen on 13 May 1969 has a more famous parallel at the level of the individual in the phenomenon of *amok*.

The phrase "to run amok" refers in colloquial English to an act of wanton unruly behaviour. The first account of it is from fifteenth century Indonesia. It was described as a condition or phenomenon that is associated with the Malay people (Hatta 1996, p. 505). E. K. Tan and John E. Carr describe *amok* as

> a standardized form of intense emotional release, accepted by the community and expected of any male individual who is placed for some reason or other in an intolerably embarrassing or shameful situation. The indiscriminate killings are considered a continuation of revengeful feelings. ... The Amok must re-establish himself in the eyes of his fellow man and proceeds to do so by a "violent assertion of his power" — the only court of appeal known to his fathers for countless generations (1977, p. 59).

The violence associated with an *amok* episode is simultaneously regarded as being indiscriminate and yet purposive and revengeful. Carr and Tan note that the subjects aver "that the act is unconscious, indiscriminate, and without purpose", but that several of those who had run *amok* "exhibited a remarkable degree of purposiveness" (1976, p. 1297). One subject they noted had killed five Chinese in three separate coffee houses frequented by Chinese and he had previously expressed anger towards the Chinese for the 1969 riots (ibid.). All accounts of *amok* describe the role of the *amok* in restoring lost dignity or in saving face (see ibid.; Kon 1994).

The violent riots of 1969 may appear to be a social manifestation of Malay *amok* (cf. van Dijk 2002). Indeed, this association was made explicit by Mahathir Mohamad. In a widely circulated letter to the then Prime Minister, Tunku Abdul Rahman, Mahathir criticized him for "giving the Chinese what they demand. ... The Malays have run amok, killing those they hate because you have given them too much face" (quoted in Munro-Kua 1996, p. 56). I might note that the *amok* phenomenon is frequently regarded as being born of culturally emphasized courtesy and self-effacement which "may lead others, interpreting such diffidence as weakness and inferiority, to take advantage of [the Malay]" (Carr and Tan 1976, p. 1298).

Sir Stamford Raffles (1781–1826) noted that the threat of *amok* protects the Malays. He wrote that the Malay was "prepared to avenge with the *kris* [traditional dagger] the slightest insult on the spot; but with the knowledge that such an immediate appeal is always at hand, prevents the necessity of its often being resorted to" (quoted in Hatta 1996, p. 506; for more, see Lee 2007, pp. 59–62).

In recent times the idea of *amok* and the symbol of the *kris* has been invigorated in ostensible defence of Malay rights. In the UMNO general assembly of 2006, Mohamad Rahmat said to the assembly, but directing the comment to non-Malays, "Don't test the Malays, they know 'amok'". Hasnoor Sidang Hussein similarly stated, "UMNO is willing to risk lives and bathe in blood in defence of race and religion". Notoriously at this same assembly, Hishamuddin Hussein unsheathed and kissed a *kris*, an act which was widely regarded as ethnically provocative (see Noor 2006).

FROM ANWAR IBRAHIM TO
THE 2008 GENERAL ELECTIONS

The threat of ethnic violence should Malay hegemony be challenged does not work well when the challenge comes from other Malays. The framework of Islam has been used by some Malays as a framework within which to criticize the government and status quo. A significant leader of this Islamic activism was Anwar Ibrahim

In 1972, Anwar Ibrahim, a prominent student activist, founded Angkatan Belia Islam Malaysia (Islamic Youth Movement of Malaysia).[2] For some, he became "the standard bearer for Malay nationalism and Islamic fundamentalism" (Stewart 2003, p. 12). For being a leader of student demonstrations in support of poor farmers in 1974, he was detained for the first time under the ISA for more than a year.

Despite having connections with PAS, he joined UMNO in 1982 after being invited by Mahathir Mohamad. He rose quickly within UMNO and held a succession of key portfolios. His aggressiveness in seeking power, notes Ian Stewart, made him enemies who would later play a role during his sacking and trial (ibid., p. 15).

In 1993 Anwar contested and won the post of Deputy Prime Minister. Although Anwar made an unsuccessful attempt to take the Prime Minstership from Dr Mahathir in 1996, the Asian economic crisis which began in 1997 gave him a new opportunity. He was, however, sacked in September 1998. This was followed by his second detention under the ISA and eventual arrest for engaging in sodomy (a charge widely regarded as fabricated for political reasons). Between his sacking and his detention he addressed popular demonstrations against the government that were a response to the economic crisis and perceived government corruption including bail-outs of politically connected companies. The most notable demonstration that occurred at this time, and which Anwar addressed, reportedly involved over

40,000 people who converged on the National Mosque in Kuala Lumpur on 20 September 1998.

Meredith Weiss and Saliha Hassan describe the sacking of Anwar as launching the massive popular protest movement known as *Reformasi* (Reformation). Reformasi, write Weiss and Hassan,

> brought unprecedented numbers of Malaysians on to the streets and into opposition parties and NGOs. All of a sudden, the issue of people's right to participate in political activities became a top priority even in generally apathetic sections of society. Moreover, the terms of pro-democratic civil society – judicial independence, executive interference, administrative transparency, freedom of information, freedom of expression, responsible media, civil liberties and human rights — quickly became household words (Weiss and Hassan 2004, p. 12).

The events of Reformasi were responsible for the political conscientization of many Malaysians.

Yet despite the popular protests, the Mahathir-led ruling coalition won the 1999 general elections and even retained its two-thirds majority of parliamentary seats. The period subsequent to those elections saw the retirement of Mahathir and ascension of Abdullah Ahmad Badawi to the Prime Ministership. Although the fervour of the Reformasi movement waned in this period, Weiss notes that a large segment of the Malaysian population had by then become sympathetic to the causes of NGOs and to human rights ideas, and this segment would be more be more easily aroused in future (Weiss 2004, p. 163).

In the 2004 elections, the BN coalition won 90 per cent of the parliamentary seats, owing in large part to the popularity of Abdullah with his image of being "Mr Clean" and his promise to conduct an anti-corruption drive. However, between the 2004 and 2008 elections, there was apparent growing dissatisfaction regarding his leadership for numerous reasons including, but not limited to, the failures of his anti-corruption drive, his royal commission into the police force which yielded no perceivable results, and a pervasive notion that he was "sleepy-headed" while his controversial son-in-law, Khairy Jamaluddin, actually ran the country.

In 2007 several significant public protests took place which were all roundly condemned by the government. One of these took place in September in Putrajaya, Malaysia's administrative capital, principally by members of the Malaysian Bar in protest at apparent corrupt practices concerning the judiciary (Malaysian Bar 2007). This was followed in November by the 30,000 to 40,000 strong Bersih (Clean) rally in Kuala

Lumpur which ended in a memorandum being submitted to the Sultan. This memorandum called for the introduction of several practices to increase the fairness and transparency of general elections (see Chapter 8). Later in November 2007 another demonstration was organized by the Hindu Rights Action Force (HINDRAF) to protest the poor social condition of Indians in Malaysia. This 30,000 or so strong rally was met with a heavy-handed response by police and saw several HINDRAF leaders detained without trial under the ISA and dozens of ralliers charged with attempted murder (Ooi, Saravanamuttu, and Lee 2008, p. 12). Whereas the Bersih rally was largely not reported in the mainstream media — except for mentions of traffics jams in Kuala Lumpur that day — the HINDRAF rally was vilified and pictures portrayed the ralliers negatively. The front page of the *New Straits Times*, for example, featured a photo of a rallier hurling away a tear-gas canister that had been fired into the crowd.

Despite the vilifications, however, the sentiments expressed by the HINDRAF ralliers on 25 November appeared to have traction in the Indian community. This movement was a likely cause of the swing of the Indian vote away from the BN of about 35 per cent in the 2008 general elections (Ong 2008; see also Ooi, Saravanamuttu, and Lee 2008, p. 41). This swing was echoed across the other ethnic groups in Malaysia to smaller degrees — Chinese 30 per cent and Malay 5 per cent — and cumulating in what was popularly described as a "political tsunami". This "tsunami" swept away dozens of BN incumbents and removed the coalition's two-thirds majority in Parliament for the first time since 1969. It also saw PKR, which is closely associated with Anwar Ibrahim, become the largest opposition party in Parliament. Furthermore, five state assemblies fell under the control of the coalition of opposition parties on 8 March — the largest number of states ever to not be under BN control.

The activism which I principally examine in this book took place during the Prime Ministership of Abdullah Badawi and so examines the interplay between authoritarianism, Islam, and activism in the post-Mahathir era up until the Prime Ministership of Najib Tun Razak which began on 3 April 2009. The natural book-ends for my discussion are thus the general elections that took place in 2004 and 2008. However, the political history preceding 2004 is of course critical in understanding contemporary Malaysian politics and Islam and so is liberally referred to here. One discourse of unequivocal importance which gained significant ground and legitimacy during the Mahathir era, and which greatly conditioned the activism that took place during the Abdullah era, was that of the Islamic state, which I examine in the following chapter.

Notes

1. The details of Islamization in Malaysia's early period are beyond the scope of this book which concentrates on the dynamics of politicized Islam in the period between 2003 to 2008. The earlier history of Islamization has been treated in greater depth by others such as Mutalib (1990 and 1993), Nagata (1984), and Noor (2004).

2. For more on the work which Anwar's organization Angkatan Belia Islam Malaysia undertook in promoting Islam to Malay youth, as well as the work of other Islamic proselytizing groups, see Zainah (1987).

3

MALAYSIA AS AN ISLAMIC STATE
The Debate

Of the arguments in the Islamic state debate that I explore in this chapter, first are those that should be regarded as emanating from UMNO and the Islamization mechanisms that it has established. Among these arguments are that existing political structures are in some way already Islamic or consistent with Islam and that Malaysia ought to undergo a process of further Islamization.

Second, I examine the approach of liberal constitutionalists who interpret Malaysia's Constitution as being fundamentally liberal and not suggestive of an Islamic state. As an exemplar of this approach I take the position articulated by lawyer Malik Imtiaz Sarwar who directly refutes the government position. Third, I turn to PAS. PAS wishes to turn Malaysia into an Islamic state and disputes UMNO's assertion that Malaysia already is.

One point of interest in these three perspectives is the different historical groundings employed to legitimize the different positions. UMNO's salient historical foundation is the imagined history of the Malaysian peninsula in which Islamic law prevailed prior to both colonialism and the immigration of Chinese and Indian migrants. The temporal precedence of the Malays also forms a key historical justification for UMNO's arguments that Malaysia is an Islamic state and ought to be regarded as such. For liberal constitutionalists, the salient historical foundation is the creation of Malaysia's Constitution which embodies and articulates The Bargain.

The Constitution is regarded as essentially liberal and forms the legitimate contemporary legal and political framework by which personal liberties and freedoms should be reckoned. For PAS, on the other hand, the salient historical foundation is Medina under the leadership of the Prophet Muhammad. The constitution of Medina which was created by Muhammad forms a model for PAS as it was multi-religious and multi-ethnic like Malaysia is today. However, although its salient historical model is the oldest of the three, PAS's vision is forward-looking in that it is less interested in interpreting the current Constitution or restoring Malaysia's past, but seeks to posit a completely new Constitution for Malaysia. Instead of the 1957 Constitution, the primary sources of legislation for PAS are to be the Quran and the *Sunnah* (traditions of the Prophet).

THE PERSPECTIVE OF UMNO

On 29 September 2001, Mahathir Mohamad announced that Malaysia was already an Islamic state at the Annual General Assembly of the ostensibly multi-ethnic but Chinese-dominated BN component party, Gerakan. Strong objections to this announcement soon followed from various quarters. Many non-Muslims and Muslims alike objected because they regarded Malaysia as liberal and, in effect, secular. Conservative Muslims, such as those from PAS, also objected. The ostensible reason for their objections included that many of the characteristics of an Islamic state, in particular the Hudud laws and punishments (see below), were absent. Politically though, if PAS accepted that Malaysia was an Islamic state, the party would lose much of its reason for being (see Martinez 2005, p. 151).

In defence of the declaration, the Ministry of Information's Department of Special Affairs published a booklet. It was titled *Malaysia Adalah Sebuah Negara Islam* (Malaysia is an Islamic State). This booklet was later withdrawn from circulation, almost certainly owing to the criticism it drew. Nevertheless, the justifications and legitimizations of Mahathir's claim remain important as they are common justifications for regarding Malaysia as an Islamic state.

Among the justifications detailed in this booklet are four scholars' definitions of an Islamic state which Malaysia is said to fulfil. These definitions are:

1. Sayikh Muhammad Abu Zuhrah: "An Islamic State is a state under the authority or rule of an Islamic government; the power and defence of the state are in the hands of the followers of Islam. Such a state must be defended by every Muslim."

2. Muhammad bin Hasan Al-Syaibani: "A state, which is ruled by followers of Islam and where Muslims are able to live in peace."

3. Imam Al-Fahistani: "An Islamic State is a state where Islamic administrative law is enforced (Islamic law is enforced)."

4. Imam Syafi'i: "Any state that was an Islamic state will not lose its Islamic status under the *fiqh Islam*, even if the followers of Islam in that state have been defeated. This means that Islamic republics, which are currently under communist rule or other powers, are considered Islamic States that have been colonised, and it is the responsibility of the followers of Islam to free these states when they are able to" (cited in Christian Federation of Malaysia 2002, pp. 10–11; parentheses original).

The author of *Malaysia Adalah Sebuah Negara Islam*, Wan Zahid Wan Teh, is also aware that one of the defining characteristics of an Islamic state is not among the above definitions. That characteristic is the presence of the Hudud laws. Hudud is the plural of *Hadd*, which is the Arabic word for "limit". It refers in orthodox Islamic law to specific punishments for six specific crimes. Those crimes are apostasy (*riddah*), armed robbery (*hirbah*), theft (*sariqah*), drinking alcohol (*shurb*), adultery (*zinna*), and false accusation of adultery (*qadhf*). The punishments include death by stoning (for adultery and apostasy) and the severing of the hand (for theft). Sunni orthodoxy holds that the four main jurists — Maliki, Hanbali, Hanafi and Shafi'i — all agreed that *ijtihad* (Islamic legal reasoning) led to the conclusion that, in Islam, these punishments were mandatory for these crimes. However, the booklet explains that

> the requirements to govern an Islamic state are vast and not just confined to implementing hudud laws only. ... [I]t is neither logical nor justifiable to consider implementation of the hudud laws alone as the basis for determining as to whether the Government is Islamic or not (ibid.).

It goes on to explain that the Malaysian government has, overall, fulfilled its Islamic responsibilities despite weaknesses which are being improved. It goes on to say, "Since the contemporary system of governance has been inherited from the colonial power, there are some prevailing rules and regulations that do not suit the requirements of Islam" (ibid.). Owing to this,

> the Government has launched the policy [of] "Absorption of Islamic Values" in the administration of the Government. Through this policy, everything that contradicts Islam will be realigned to conform to the needs of Islam step by step in ways that are wise. ... It is a policy that will be

implemented step by step until the goal of entrenching Islam into the nation's system is fully achieved (ibid.).

In accordance with the government's policy of the "Absorption of Islamic Values", the Ahmad Ibrahim Kulliyyah (Faculty) of Laws at the International Islamic University of Malaysia established in 2002 its "Harmonisation of Shari'ah and Law Unit" (HSLU). This committee attempts to oversee and organize programmes to explore how existing law in Malaysia can be brought into consonance with Syariah law (Kamali 2003*a*).

"The basic frame of reference for the HSLU should be to encourage Shari'ah related research that aim (sic) at bringing harmony between the *Shari'ah* and civil law" (Kamali 2003*a*, p. 154; italics original). As an example of a suggested project for this unit, Mohammad Hashim Kamali reports that "[c]ertain provisions of the Malaysian Penal Code may be revised in order to utilize the resources of Islamic law and ensure overall harmony with Islamic principles" (ibid., p. 155). He goes on to note that "[t]he Penal Code is silent, for example, on illicit cohabitation among non-Muslims. The *khalwat* provisions that are currently found in the State Enactments of Malaysia are also not applied to non-Muslims" (ibid., p. 155).

Although harmonization may imply a process by which two separate legal traditions may be mutually informing and edifying, it is clear that, for the most part, harmonizing in the contemporary context entails Islamizing (cf. Roff 1998, p. 211). Indeed, Kamali reports that the HSLU "was initially called the Islamisation of Law Committee" (ibid., p. 151). "Islamisation" was replaced with "Harmonisation" because the former was seen as too unilateral and was the subject of "suspicion" by non-Muslims. "Harmonisation is not expected to invoke the same criticism that was levelled at 'Islamisation'" (Kamali 2003*b*, p. 3).

However, in view of the demographic and parliamentary composition of Malaysia, Abdul Aziz Bari suggested in a paper presented at the International Conference on Harmonisation of Shariah and Civil Law in 2003 which was organized by the HSLU, that amending the Constitution to acknowledge the Quran and *Sunnah* as the supreme sources of law may be impossible. However, he goes on to suggest that

> one might argue that although Islam has not been recognized as a formal source of law it may become the spirit that guides and directs the system; standing in the background and guiding the direction of the system. In other words Islamic principles or Islam-inspired ideas may form the substance of statutes and policies without being declared as such. In a multi-racial country like Malaysia this seems to be a more viable formula for Islamization (ibid., p. 8).

It is clear from this passage, as well as the comments of other Islamists, that the role of non-Muslims in the construction or amendment of Malaysian civil law has been ignored, or at best marginalized. When Bari suggests modifying Malaysia's laws and Constitution "to restore the old glory" of the country's pre-colonial period (ibid., p. 1), it is clear that the vision for Malaysia's future, couched in an image of a past before most Chinese and Indians arrived, leaves these populations out.

I should note that the International Islamic University of Malaysia was part of Mahathir's Islamization policy (see also Noor 2004, p. 376). Another element of this policy was the establishment of the Institut Kefahaman Islam Malaysia (IKIM, or Malaysian Institute of Islamic Understanding). IKIM is a research institute situated in Kuala Lumpur which produces material that frequently legitimizes the actions of the government from an Islamic perspective. It produces a journal, the *IKIM Journal of Islam and International Affairs*. In 2003 it published an article that also sought to justify Mahathir's declaration that Malaysia was an Islamic state. The author, Abdul Rashid Moten, a lecturer at the International Islamic University of Malaysia, makes a number of notable arguments. These arguments highlight points of contention between those who view Malaysia as an Islamic state and those who do not.

One argument of particular note made by Moten is that the first Prime Minister of Malaysia, Tunku Abdul Rahman, sought to establish Malaysia as an Islamic state (Moten 2003, pp. 1–2). The author claims, however, that Abdul Rahman was "justifiably preoccupied with ensuring national security and maintaining racial harmony" and thus, "while encouraging the ritualistic and symbolic aspects of Islam, he was careful not to publicly declare his interest in establishing an Islamic state" (ibid., p. 2).

Moten directly asks the question, "Is Malaysia secular?" (ibid., p. 28). He notes that neither in the Constitution nor in the landmark judgement in the case of *Che Omar bin Che Soh* (in which the court described Islam's constitutional role as relating *only* to State ceremonies) is it stated positively that Malaysia is secular. Also, according to Moten, no comments ever made by the first Prime Minister or the Reid Commission, which drafted the Constitution, have ever asserted that Malaysia is or was to be positively secular.

Moten also cites characteristics of contemporary Malaysia in support of the positive Islamic nature of Malaysia. These include that elections have been "reasonably fair", that access to media during elections is sufficiently free as "[t]he opposition has full access to its own papers, the Internet and a busy foreign press", and that the "government has avoided any systematic deployment of goons and 'muscle-men' to menace supporters [of the opposition]". Other claims include that "the poor are provided with comfortable houses", that tensions between the government and interest groups arise only when these groups "insist on operating outside the framework of co-operation, trust and responsibility", and the government only resorts to security acts when "activists 'go too far.'" Moten also claims that use of the ISA is confined to the preservation of peace including on such occasions as in 1987 (Operasi Lalang) and 1998 (Reformasi).

Some of the purported characteristics of Malaysia cited above are commonplace in clearly non-Islamic countries. Thus a further important claim to support construing Malaysia as an Islamic state that is sometimes made is that Islamic law was ubiquitous in Malaysia prior to colonization. Malaysia as an Islamic state is thus a *return* to that prior condition. This position is taken by the late Universiti Malaya Dean of Law, and Islamic International University Shaykh al Kulliyyah of Laws, Ahmad Ibrahim, who, as will be seen in Chapter 5, used this claim to make a technical legal argument in support of the primacy of Islamic law over Malaysia's Constitution.

As mentioned earlier, there are many who strenuously deny that Malaysia is or should be an Islamic state. Many of these voices are those of non-Muslims. The DAP strongly condemned Mahathir's declaration on 29 September 2001 and launched a "Say 'No' to 929" campaign. Interestingly, it would appear that Tunku Abdul Rahman is on the DAP's side on this issue. He said,

> After all these years of trying to build a genuine multiracial and multi-religious Malaysia, we are now confronted with a new danger — Islamic fundamentalism … they are now raising all kinds of ideas to Islamise the country, and this is not good (in Fernando 2002, p. 218; see Photo 1 in this volume).

Civil society groups and activists have also disputed UMNO's construal of Malaysia as an Islamic state and have defended a liberal reading of the Constitution. One proponent of such a reading is Malik Imtiaz Sarwar. In the past Malik has taken on a number of cases relating to freedom of religion in Malaysia, is one of Malaysia's most high-profile constitutional lawyers, and is a significant voice in the *Article 11* coalition described in Chapter 6. I examine next his views as they were propounded at a conference held by Malaysia's official human rights body, Suruhanjaya Hak Asasi Manusia Malaysia (Suhakam, or The Human Rights Commission of Malaysia).

MALIK IMTIAZ SARWAR ON MALAYSIA AS
A LIBERAL CONSTITUTIONAL STATE

On 9 and 10 September 2004 Suhakam organized in Kuala Lumpur a two-day conference titled "Human Rights and Good Governance". At this conference Malik delivered a paper on freedom from discrimination. In this paper he described how political Islam and the idea that Malaysia is an Islamic state has resulted in discrimination.

Malik told the audience, which was made up of journalists, interested lay people, Suhakam staff, and representatives of other countries' embassies, that Suhakam had requested from the government a statement regarding Malaysia's status as an Islamic state. He went on to say,

> [The request was] met with this wholly self serving response: Malaysia is an Islamic State because:-
>
> a. the nation was founded by Muslims;
> b. the Head of the Nation is a, and the government is in the hands of, Muslim(s);
> c. the majority of its citizenry are Muslims and most of their cultural and social elements are influenced by the culture of Islam;
> d. the Islamic *ummah* (in Malaysia) are free to abide by Islamic Law and are even supported in this regard by the Government;
> e. systems to increase religious observance of "*munakahat*" (religious rules pertaining to marriage) and "*muamalat*" (rules pertaining to societal issues) are implemented all over the nation;
> f. Islamic education is taught from primary school to the tertiary education level and its quality is continuously being improved;
> g. the existence of Shari'ah courts and Shari'ah laws; and
> h. the existence of other Islamic institutions which expand the greatness of Islam.
>
> Besides the above, Malaysia satisfies several other criteria that shows it is an Islamic state, namely:
>
> i. provision in the Federal Constitution which provides that the religion of Islam is the religion of the Federation (Article 3(1)), Head of State as Head of the religion of Islam (Article 3(2), (3) and (5)) and administration of Islamic matters being the responsibility of the state government and federal government (Article 74);
> j. global recognition of Malaysia as an Islamic state; and
> k. most of the provisions in the Constitution are not contrary to Islam.[1]

Malik expressed concern over the "re-casting of historical fact", asking, "At which point in time was this country founded by Muslims? And where does our constitutional history fit into the discourse?"

Many liberal constitutionalists and lawyers, such as Malik, take as their salient historical reference the 1957 Constitution. A nation's constitution is its supreme law and sets out its legal framework. It also says something of the character of the nation, outlining those values or principles that take precedence over others.

During an interview, Malik explained to me that there are basically two approaches to constitutional interpretation. First, there was the literal approach which required that the precise, pedantic meaning of a word or statement was what was accepted as what the law meant. A second interpretative approach, Malik related to me, required that a given article be interpreted with the context and purpose of its creation in mind. This, the purposive approach, was that normally taken in interpreting constitutions, but also with lesser laws. He said that according to this approach it was clear that the "Constitution was meant to be a secular Constitution and the role of Islam was meant to be for ceremonial purposes only." In contradiction to Abdul Rashid Moten, Malik referred to the Reid Commission report which stated that although the religion of Malaysia shall be Islam, this "shall not imply that the State is not a secular state" (see also Sheridan and Groves 2004, p. 33). Malik also cited the decision in the case of *Che Omar bin Che Soh* in which the judges found that Islam played only a ceremonial role in Malaysia and does not influence the validity of Malaysia's criminal law (see also Bari and Shuaib 2004, pp. 6–7).

Malik's question at the Suhakam seminar, "At what point was this nation founded by Muslims?" was in effect an argument that there was really no construal of "the nation" to which "was founded by Muslims" could be accurately applied in Malaysia's case. It is well accepted that indigenous Malaysians had and often still maintain a traditional (non-Muslim) cosmology of beliefs. Among those people who arrived after the indigenous Malaysians, and who became known as the Malays, a Hindu cosmology prevailed prior to the spread of Islam (Syed N.A. 1969).

At the Suhakam conference, Malik identified "political Islam" as "the biggest threat this nation faces". He went on to say that "it is insidiously insinuating itself into most, if not all, aspects of our life". Describing political Islam as an obsession with labels, Malik argued that describing Malaysia as Islamic is inherently divisive and suggests superiority in as much as it suggests inferiority. He described those propounding these labels as having "led us to the brink of a precipice [and] have in turn led us to a divided society". Among the effects of Islamization, Malik mentioned how Islamic prayers start the day at most schools' morning assemblies, how some schools ban the use of shorts by girls, and how others have banned the consumption of non-halal food by students of all faiths. Such acts, according to Malik, send a "loud and clear" message to non-Muslims that they do not share an equal place with Muslims in Malaysia.

PAS'S CONSTRUAL OF MALAYSIA AS AN ISLAMIC STATE

Whereas UMNO's approach has been to Islamize Malaysia, PAS desires to establish an Islamic order anew. In analysing PAS's position, the most pertinent reference is its "Islamic State Document" which was first released in 2003 (Parti Islam SeMalaysia 2004).

The document begins by citing an "Islamic maxim" that states, "If an obligatory act can only be performed with the availability of a specific item, then the procurement of that item is equally obligatory." In the context of this document, PAS is suggesting that to lead a properly Muslim life, it is obligatory to live in an Islamic state. The form of this Islamic state appears inspired by the "Constitution of Medina, known as 'Sahifah Medina'". In the document's preamble, it notes that "[t]he first Islamic State was established in the multi-racial, multi-cultural and multi-religious society of Medina in the period of the Prophet and the Rightly Guided Caliphates and so shall it need to be established till the end of time".

The document asserts that a particular prayer[2] said by Muslims "is meaningless unless its true demands are earnestly fulfilled" and thus "it is imperative that a true Islamic state be established". The document also states that "Islam is the solution to all human problems including issues arising from plural society". The states of Kelantan and Terengganu (which PAS governed between 1999 and 2004) are cited as having borne the fruit of establishing Islam in governance and administration under PAS's rule.

PAS's document distinguishes differences between what it regards as a "true Islamic state" and a "pseudo Islamic state". One such difference relates to sovereignty. "The Islamic State has an absolute sovereign Who cannot be challenged or interfered with. Absolute sovereignty belongs to Allah Almighty as He is the creator and hence the Provider and Source of Laws." Man's position is that of vicegerent whose duties are that of "guardianship over the religion of Islam and administering the state according to its teachings".

PAS's Islamic state is one in which "the Holy Quran and the Prophetic Tradition (As-Sunnah) [are] the primary sources of legislation". Because this legislation is based "on the laws of the Almighty Who is Most Gracious and Most Merciful", "[i]t is impossible for these laws to be the cause or source of injustice". The document notes that "[m]an-made laws have been proven a failure in guaranteeing the security and dignity of the human race". Syariah law necessarily includes the Hudud punishments, the implementation of which "provides the much required peace and security as crimes would be reduced to a minimum".

I should note that during their administration of Kelantan and Terengganu, PAS passed the "Syariah Criminal Code (II) Bill" and the "Syariah Criminal Offences (Hudud and Qisas) Bill" in 1993 and 2002 respectively. These bills would have enforced the Hudud punishments for various crimes including stoning to death for adultery by a married person, crucifixion for armed robbery when accompanied by killing, and amputation of the right hand for a first offence of theft and of the leg for a second offence. Also, a Muslim accused of apostasy and who does not repent in three days may be killed. However, as the punishments exceed those constitutionally allowed for state laws, the bills have never been implemented (for a fuller account of the Kelantan bill, see Kamali 1995).

THREE VISIONS OF MALAYSIA

Two of the three visions described here are set within an ostensibly Islamic framework and give Islam and Muslims precedence within the nation. As mentioned earlier, much of UMNO's Islamic agenda is the result of the apparent popularity of PAS (see Chapter 8) and UMNO's need to co-opt the legitimacy that PAS found in its use of its Islamicized discourse. As Judith Nagata has noted, "It is the presence of PAS that keeps the UMNO party, the driving force of the incumbent government, constantly on the alert as to its religious credentials. If necessary, UMNO is ready to fight PAS Islam with more Islam of its own" (1997, p. 144).

Both UMNO and PAS spell out an Islamicized vision of Malaysia. UMNO, a Malay chauvinist party, articulates this vision in terms of the history of the peninsula, the Malay people and their religion. It is the temporal precedence of the Malays that justifies the Islamic vision. PAS, however, now eschews ethnic chauvinism. Unlike UMNO it has no ethnic requirements for party membership but has instead religious restrictions (though in the 2008 general elections, and undoubtedly to capture the Indian protest vote following the HINDRAF rally, the party made history by fielding its first non-Muslim candidate, Kumutha Rahman, a twenty-nine year old female law graduate). Despite also dropping the establishment of an Islamic state as a key platform in 2008, there can be little doubt that this remains a long-term objective, but one which appeared unpragmatic after PAS's poor showing at the 2004 elections (see Chapter 8). The objective of making Malaysia an Islamic state is rationalized more on the grounds of the demographic preponderance of Muslims in Malaysia as a contemporary fact rather than to repair the history of Malaysia as an Islamic country which was wrongly interrupted by colonialism, which is frequently the discourse of UMNO.

The currency of the Islamic discourse in Malaysian politics has been demonstrated on more than one occasion when UMNO and PAS exchanged charges of *kafir* (unbeliever) to delegitimize each other and to attempt to claim the position of the authentically Islamic party (see Kamarulnizam 2003, pp. 194–95; Nagata 1997, p. 144). This effort to claim the position of Islamic authenticity has led to mutual attempts at out-Islamizing each other. The effects of the overall legitimacy of Islam in public discourse has had consequences on the ways many people live their lives in Malaysia. In the following chapter, I describe the difficulties that would-be apostates have in officially leaving Islam and thus also turn to the first set of Malaysia's activists that I examine in this book, lawyers.

Notes

1. Quotations from Malik's presentation are taken from a privately circulated copy of the text.
2. According to this document, this prayer reads, "Truly, my prayer, my worship, my life and my death is only for Allah, Master and Cherisher of the entire Universe."

4

CONFLICT OF JURISDICTION
Civil versus Syariah Law

This chapter explores the legal contest over the interpretation of two articles of Malaysia's Constitution: Article 3, which declares that "Islam is the religion of the federation", and Article 11, which outlines the liberty of freedom of religion. The prism through which this contest is examined is the case of Lina Joy, a woman who wished to officially change her religion from Islam to Christianity.

Lina Joy's series of hearings from the High Court through to the highest court of the land[1] attracted a great deal of (often heated) public attention and spawned the freedom of religion movement described in Chapter 6. Her case crystallized the debate over whether Malaysia was fundamentally guided by a liberal interpretation of the Constitution or by Islamic orthodoxy. If Lina Joy was to be given the right to convert to Christianity without hindrance, as her counsel argued she ought to be, Malaysia could be seen as secular. If she was prevented from so doing, or required the consent of the Syariah courts, Islam could be regarded as forming the framework of Malaysian politics and law.

While she lost her final hearing in the Federal Court on 30 May 2007, the discourses deployed during her case tell us a great deal about the legal and political climate in contemporary Malaysia. I recount below one particular day of a hearing in the Court of Appeal. A point of interest is the response of this woman's counsel when the broader constitutional approach, in which a liberal interpretation of Article 11 was defended, was coldly received by the judges. When this occurred, her counsel turned to a technical argument founded on a legal loophole which I examine. I should note here that the readers' comprehension of these legal arguments is not necessary for understanding the broader points of three lawyers whose views on the particular laws in question in the case I later recount.

THE CASE OF LINA JOY

Lina Joy was born to Muslim parents and named Azlina binte Jailani. On 21 February 1997, when she was thirty-three years old, she applied to the National Registration Department (NRD) in Malaysia to have her name changed from Azlina binte Jailani to Lina Lelani. This was intended to indicate her conversion from Islam. She had also stated in an affidavit that she had converted to Christianity and had been baptized in a church. She also intended to marry a Christian man. After her application was rejected by the NRD she applied again to have her name changed to Lina Joy. She also applied to have the word "Islam" removed from her new identity card (known as a MyKad) (Faiza 2004, p. 119).

Her applications for a change of name from a Muslim name to a non-Muslim name and for the removal of the word "Islam" from her MyKad were rejected by the NRD because these would have indicated that she had left Islam. The NRD deemed that because she is a Muslim, she required a letter from the Syariah court to affirm or declare that she was no longer a Muslim. It is worth noting briefly here that the Syariah court is a state and territory level court because the administration of the affairs of Muslims in Malaysia is controlled at the state and territory level. Each state and territory has a different set of Syariah laws which are legislated by the relevant parliaments.

Lina Joy's applications were made in the territory of Kuala Lumpur which is subject to the Syariah Criminal Offences Act 1997. Although this Act does not list apostasy as an offence, one who wished to convert from Islam could be regarded as committing the offence of *takfir*. *Takfir* is the making of an accusation that a person or group of persons is either (1) a non-Muslim, (2) has ceased to profess Islam, (3) should not or cannot be accepted as professing the Islamic religion, or (4) does not believe, follow, profess or belong to the Islamic religion (Kairos 2004, p. 42). Lina Joy's lawyers argued that she should be able to change her religion without hindrance as per her right as a Malaysian under Article 11 of the Constitution.

As noted in the previous chapter, how Malaysia's Constitution is to be interpreted is disputed. Of particular pertinence are Articles 3 and 11. This chapter and the following examine the legal and social contest over the meaning of these Articles, in particular by lawyers who, on the one side, advocate for a liberal interpretation, and on the other, by those who argue for a more restrictive interpretation that is in closer accord with Islamic orthodoxy.

LINA JOY'S CASE IN THE HIGH COURT

Although the NRD demanded a letter from the Syariah court, Lina Joy refused to apply there because she no longer considered herself a Muslim and thus had no standing in the Malaysian Syariah courts which only have jurisdiction over Muslims. As importantly perhaps, she had engaged in activities that could be construed by the courts as bringing Islam into disrepute. She therefore made an application to the High Court of Kuala Lumpur for a number of declaratory orders. The effect of these orders was to affirm her right to freedom of religion under Article 11 and to declare Syariah laws that limited this freedom as null and void.

Article 11 of the Constitution is found in the section that addresses the fundamental liberties of the individual. Article 11 reads:

11. (1) Every person has the right to profess and practice his religion and, subject to Clause (4), to propagate it.
    (2) No person shall be compelled to pay any tax the proceeds of which are specifically allocated in whole or in part for the purposes of a religion other than his own.
    (3) Every religious group has the right —
        (a) to manage its own religious affairs;
        (b) to establish and maintain institutions for religious or charitable purposes; and
        (c) to acquire and own property and hold and administer it in accordance with law.
    (4) State law and in respect of the Federal Territories of Kuala Lumpur, Labuan and Putrajaya, federal law may control or restrict the propagation of any religious doctrine or belief among persons professing the religion of Islam.
    (5) This Article does not authorize any act contrary to any general law relating to public order, public health or morality.

Lina Joy lost her case in the High Court. Of interest, however, is the judge's interpretation of Article 11, because, in this case and others, it is apparent that Syariah law is becoming increasingly powerful and arguably more so than the Constitution.

In essence, Lina Joy's applications were dismissed because she was deemed by the court to still be a Muslim regardless of any action intended to indicate otherwise. Although Article 11 states that, "[e]very person has the right to profess and practice his religion", the judge found that this does not mean that Lina Joy "was to be given the freedom of choice to profess and practice the religion of her choice" (Faiza 2004, p. 120). In other words, the judge decided that Article 11 confers upon citizens the right to profess their religion, but not necessarily the right to *choose* which religion is theirs to profess.

Lina Joy's counsel compared Article 11 of Malaysia's Constitution with the comparable article in the Indian Constitution. Article 25 of the Indian Constitution is explicit about citizens' freedom to choose their religion. Article 25(1) of the Indian Constitution states that "… all persons are equally entitled to freedom of conscience and the right to freely profess, practice and propagate religion". Freedom of conscience, this Constitution tells us, refers to the "absolute inner freedom of the citizen to mould his own relation with god in whatever manner he pleases" (Faiza 2004, p. 130). The court noted that the phrase "freedom of conscience" and "freely profess" were absent in the Malaysian Constitution and were not implied. Furthermore, the equivalency of the Malaysian Constitution with the Indian Constitution could not be sustained because the Indian Constitution did not contain provisions equivalent to Articles 3(1), 12, 121(1A) and 160.[2]

These provisions were deemed by the court to indicate that the Malaysian Constitution is not secular and are seen by those who construe Malaysia as an Islamic state as affirming that Malaysia is not a secular state. These articles also affirm for them that Islamically oriented interpretations of the Constitution and lesser laws are legitimate. Indeed, whereas the Indian Constitution specifically states in its preamble that India is secular, the Malaysian Constitution accords Islam a recognized position.

In the past, however, the courts have found that Islam plays no role in the interpretation of ordinary law. In the 1986 case of *Che Omar bin Che Soh vs Public Prosecutor*, the plaintiff submitted that because Article 3 states that Islam is the religion of the federation, and because the death penalty for drug trafficking and for fire-arms offences is not Islamic, the death penalty was thus unconstitutional. The court disagreed and asserted that Article 3 meant that Islam was the religion of the federation only with regard to rituals and ceremonies of State (see also Fernando 2002, p. 250).

More recently, the courts have not construed Malaysia in a secular fashion. In the High Court judgement of Lina Joy in 2001, the judge noted that Malaysia is neither secular like Singapore or India, nor theocratic like Saudi Arabia or Iran, but a hybrid. The judge was of the view that "by looking at the constitution as a whole, it is the general tenor of the constitution that Islam is given a special position and status" (Faiza 2004, p. 127). This position consequently influences the interpretation of its articles, such as Article 11 in this case.

LINA JOY'S CASE IN THE COURT OF APPEAL: THE CONSTITUTIONAL APPROACH

Lina Joy appealed the High Court's dismissal of her applications. On 14 October 2004, Lina Joy's counsel, headed by Cyrus Das, argued for his client's freedom to convert out of Islam by taking two distinct approaches. The first approach that Das presented was based on the appellant's right to freedom of religion as guaranteed under Article 11. As opposed to the "technical approach", which I will examine later, I will refer to this as the "constitutional approach".

Das argued that Article 11 does not prevent a person from changing religion or having no religion and that the restrictions that are found in Clause 4 of Article 11 refer only to the *propagation* of religion to Muslims. Referring to the previous judgement in Lina Joy's High Court hearing — that one can profess one's religion but not choose it — Das said that Article 11 should not be read in a literal manner as one would read a statute, but rather with its spirit in mind. The Reid Commission, which drafted the Constitution, made it clear that Article 3 does not change the character of Malaysia as a secular state.

In response to Das's arguments, Judge Ram said that there is freedom of religion in Malaysia, but Article 11 did not mean what Das took it to mean. Judge Ram suggested that it was active discrimination against and abuse of non-Muslims that Article 11 was drafted to avert. Furthermore, said Judge Ram, Article 11 must be subject to the personal laws of Muslims.

Das replied that personal law must be invalid if it is contrary to the Constitution. Article 11 should be read with Article 8 which states that all citizens are equal before the law and entitled to equal protection by the law. Furthermore, Article 10 ensures freedom to belong to an association as well as the freedom *not* to belong to an association. Article 10 should be read with Article 11 to mean that the right to be a member of a religion should include the right to not be a member of a religion. Any procedure that impedes the liberty to join, not join, or resign, must be invalid. Constitutional rights can only be weakened by referring to another part of the Constitution, not to law external to it.

Judge Ram at this point lamented that it appeared to him that much of the Constitution had been "written on running water". He bemoaned previous judgements that undermined the spirit of the Constitution. He lamented that every time he tried to push the Constitution forward, "we are put into reverse gear". As for Das's contention that external laws cannot weaken constitutional rights, Judge Ram referred to cases well known among Malaysian lawyers where ordinary law had overriden the Constitution (see Fritz and Flaherty 2003 for an example of constitutional weakness in the face of ordinary laws).

THE TECHNICAL APPROACH

Judge Ram's general tenor was not encouraging for Lina Joy's counsel. Das, reading Judge Ram's resistance to his constitutional approach, then took what I will refer to as the "technical approach". This approach relied on relatively minor legal points relating to the NRD's unwillingness to change Lina Joy's name and to remove the word "Islam" from her MyKad.

Das pointed out that changes of name usually must be accompanied by an explanation of the change. For example, he said, if one wished to change one's name to David Beckham, one would explain that one admires and aspires to be like the British footballer David Beckham. This necessity for an explanation, however, is not necessary when the name change is for religious reasons. If one converted from Christianity to Islam and took an Islamic name, then no explanation is required. Likewise if one converted from Hinduism to Buddhism.

On the issue of how to determine whether one has in fact converted out of Islam, Judge Ram stated that the proof required is a declaration from a Syariah court. Das disagreed and said that one must look to Article 11 which guarantees unfettered freedom of religion. To this Judge Ram responded by saying that personal law is related to matters of the state and that the procedure for converting out is the "*Soon Singh* procedure".

Das then made his technical point. In the case of *Soon Singh* which occurred in the *state* of Kedah, the courts found that the body that registers conversion into Islam was to be the body that registers conversions out of Islam. In Kedah this body was the Syariah court. Das pointed out that his client's case occurred, however, in the *territory* of Kuala Lumpur and that the administration of converts into Islam is not done by the Syariah court there, but by another body, the Majlis Agama Islam Wilayah Persekutuan (Islamic Council of the Federal Territory, hereafter referred to as the Council). The *Soon Singh* procedure relies on the State List of the Constitution which confers jurisdiction to the Syariah court. The State List is a list in the Ninth Schedule of the Constitution that outlines those matters on which state parliaments may legislate.[3] But because jurisdiction in *Soon Singh* is conferred to the Syariah *court* and not to the *Council*, and because the *Council*[4] registers conversions to Islam in the federal territory of Kuala Lumpur, the *Soon Singh* procedure does not apply in Lina Joy's case. There is no law to confer authority to either the Council or the Syariah court in Kuala Lumpur. Thus neither the Syariah court nor the Council has jurisdiction on the matter. The point is a technical and confusing one, but when it was made, Judge Ram remarked, "So *Soon Singh* seems to be working in your favour now!"

THE REPLY

Haji Sulaiman Abdullah represented the Council in Lina Joy's case. Sulaiman began by saying that he had only one point of reply. That point was that when the Constitution was written there was a clear division of the population with Malays and Muslims on the one side and, gesturing a whole being divided into two, non-Muslims on the other. All references to other countries fail because the Malaysian Constitution specifically refers to Islam and defines Malays as being Muslim.

Judge Ram surprised Sulaiman by interrupting. "Not relevant!" he said. "His client went to the registration department and wants Islam taken off and they wouldn't do it." Sulaiman replied that Lina Joy must go the Syariah court for a declaration. Sulaiman raised a case known as *Zolkaffily* (Faiza 2002). In *Zolkaffily* the court decided that Article 121(1a) of the Constitution gives exclusive jurisdiction to the Syariah court for matters listed in the State List in the Ninth Schedule. It was decided that jurisdiction was conferred to the Syariah court even if no positive law had been created by the state legislature on the given matter in the State List. When Sulaiman argued that following judicial precedent in *Zolkaffily*, the civil court loses jurisdiction on matters in the State List, the following exchange occurred:

> Judge Ram: The civil court never loses jurisdiction.
> Sulaiman: With 121(1a) it loses all jurisdiction.
> Judge Ram: Then who decides whether it is in the Syariah courts?
> Sulaiman: The civil court. But you look at the State List, not at the state enactments.

Judge Ram: 121(1a) gives power (to register conversions from Islam) to the Syariah courts, not the Majlis.

Sulaiman: But *Zolkaffily* says...

Judge Ram: But that's academic because *Zolkaffily* took place in a place where the authority was in fact the Syariah courts.

Sulaiman: It deals with the general issue. [The case of] *Mohamed Hakim*[5] also says that you don't look at the state enactments, but you look at 121(1a). That's what the decisions are saying.

Judge Ram: But 121(1a) decides on the jurisdiction to *make law*. It is an *empowering* list.[6]

Sulaiman: I beseech you to consider that whether or not the state has made laws, you have to give jurisdiction to the Syariah courts on the grounds that the law, when made, would give jurisdiction to the Syariah courts.

Judge Ram then responded to Sulaiman by alluding to the famous case in English common law of *Liversidge v Anderson* in 1941. Lord Atkin's decision in this case was contrary to the other four sitting judges. Of the interpretation of the law rendered by the other judges, Lord Atkin wrote in his famous dissenting opinion,

> I know of only one authority which might justify the suggested method of construction: "When I use a word," Humpty Dumpty said in rather a scornful tone, "it means just what I choose it to mean, neither more nor less" (quoted in Luther 1998).

In response, Sulaiman brought up another case in which it had been decided that the State List was a jurisdictional list. Judge Ram told Sulaiman that the case was wrongly decided and repeated that the State List empowers the state to make laws but it does not confer jurisdiction. "I know you are relying on precedent, Haji," the Judge said, "but what if the judgement is wholly wrong? If the judgement was that the Sun rises in the West, are we to keep saying that the Sun rises in the West?" Sulaiman replied, "With respect, your honour, that is for the Federal Court to decide." "With respect," Judge Ram replied in turn, "it is for me to decide in this court." The proceedings ended with a scheduling of the next day of hearing.

TALKING WITH MALIK IMTIAZ SARWAR AND HARIS BIN MOHAMED IBRAHIM

Some days later I had the opportunity to speak with lawyers and activists Malik Imtiaz Sarwar and Haris bin Mohamed Ibrahim. Malik had held the watching brief for the Malaysian Bar Council on the day discussed above.

Haris is a high-profile lawyer, activist, and blogger, has been long involved in freedom of religion cases, and, like Malik, is a significant voice in the *Article 11* coalition (see Chapter 6).

Both Malik and Haris explained that Lina Joy's case could not be won either by compelling the relevant state institution to permit the change of name or religion. Lina Joy needed an order from a (civil law) federal-level court because as soon as she travelled into the next state, the religious authorities could well pick her up as a Muslim. Furthermore, Haris noted, the Council does not have the power to issue any document averring a conversion of a person from Islam. "In fact," he said, "we've written to them and they've written back to say they can't do that: 'That's not in our power.'"

As for the technical approach, Malik admitted that Lina Joy's particular situation may well mean that the NRD will have to change her name and remove the word "Islam" from her MyKad. This, however, would not make her, legally or administratively, a non-Muslim. The effect would be merely cosmetic, and, as Malik put it, a "non-solution" to her problems. In his view, Das would *have* to address the constitutional issues despite the trend for civil court judges to find themselves as having no jurisdiction. He went on to explain why he felt this trend was in legal error.

First, he explained, with regard to Malays who wish to convert from Islam, it is sometimes argued that because the Constitution defines a Malay person as among other things a Muslim, a person regarded as a Malay cannot as a consequence then convert to any other faith. Malik explained that the definition of a Malay in the Constitution describes such a person for legal and administrative purposes, such as for according special privileges. There is nothing to say that a person cannot be *ethnically* Malay and a non-Muslim, he went on. Haris added that the definition of a Malay in the Constitution is only provided so that the use of "Malay" is clear *in those parts of the Constitution where it is used* and that "Malay" is not used in Article 11. Referring to the conflation of ethnic, administrative, and legal definitions, Malik opined, "They've confused the lot!"

More broadly and importantly, Malik explained that laws impeding or criminalizing apostasy are illegitimate. A law can only be made by a body competent to make that law. Competency in turn, he went on, can only be conferred by a positive law, such as one might find in a Constitution. He illustrated his point with an example. "Let's say", he told me, "I were to bring a case to the Syariah court about importing something and the judge decides that he has jurisdiction and subsequently decides the case.

If I then take the case to the High Court, the judge there will not say that he cannot now hear the case. He will say that the Syariah court should never have heard the case in the first place and that the Syariah court's decision is to be ignored. In the same way, the Syariah court cannot make laws or decide on apostasy because, firstly, Article 11 protects freedom of religion, and secondly, Syariah law as described in the State List applies only to people *professing* Islam and nowhere in the Constitution does it say that apostasy is regulated and administered by the Syariah courts." However, Malik went on to tell me, the civil courts are now finding that the Syariah courts do have jurisdiction and that regulations that were designed for administering one thing, conversion into Islam, are now deemed to function for something quite different, conversion from Islam.

THE VIEW OF SALBIAH AHMAD

Lawyer and activist Salbiah Ahmad takes a different view of the issues of the conflict of jurisdiction between the Syariah and civil courts. Salbiah argues that the purpose of Article 121(1a) of the Constitution, which gives precedence to the Syariah courts where there is a conflict of jurisdiction, should be looked at differently. In her opinion the purpose of it was not to determine jurisdiction at all. Article 121(1a) was introduced to prevent "forum-shopping"; that is, it is to stop someone who received an unfavourable judgement from the Syariah court seeking a better judgement in a civil court. The practice of forum-shopping would bring the legal system of Malaysia into disrepute.

However, as Salbiah has written, "the cases on Art. 121(1A) have evolved in a direction which may have lost sight of its original rationale" (Salbiah 2007, p. 90). In *Soon Singh*, she writes elsewhere (Salbiah 2003), the Federal Court's finding sets precedents to the effect that:

(1) In a jurisdictional challenge on conversions out of Islam, the proper court which has power to hear the matter is the Syariah Court.
(2) Freedom of religion in Article 11(1) includes the freedom not to be compelled to convert to another religion be it Islam, Hinduism or Christianity (ibid., p. 75).

She goes on to write that

[p]oint number 2 is problematic. If we are averse to compulsion in converting a person to another faith, surely we should find it similarly reprehensible to compel a person to remain in the religion. The point to be served in religious freedom is protection from coercion (ibid.).

That is, anybody who was coerced into declaring oneself as a believer of a particular religion — and accusations of coercion and deception exist (Theophilus 2005) — should not be compelled to adhere to and be bound by the tenets of that religion. Equally so, a person who was once of a particular religion — or at least was regarded as being of that religion — should not be compelled to remain in a religion in which she had no faith.

Notes

1. In ascending order of rank, the three highest courts in Malaysia are the High Court, the Court of Appeal, and the Federal Court.
2. Article 3 of the Malaysian Constitution states that "Islam is the religion of the Federation; but other religions may be practised in peace and harmony in any part of the Federation". Article 12 refers to "[r]ights in respect of education" and its second clause contains the assertion that "it shall be lawful for the Federation or a State to establish or maintain or assist in establishing or maintaining Islamic institutions or provide or assist in providing instruction in the religion of Islam and incur such expenditure as may be necessary for the purpose". Article 121 addresses the "Judicial power of the Federation" and clause (1a) states that "[t]he [High Courts] shall have no jurisdiction in respect of any matter within the jurisdiction of the Syariah courts". Finally, Article 160 includes the meanings assigned to various words and phrases used in the Constitution. One of those words is "Malay", which is defined as "a person who professes the religion of Islam, habitually speaks the Malay language [and] conforms to Malay custom".
3. The State List of the Ninth Schedule of the Constitution outlines those matters which are state matters rather than federal matters. In point 1, these include: "Islamic law and personal and family law of persons professing the religion of Islam, including the Islamic law relating to succession, testate and intestate, betrothal, marriage, divorce, dower, maintenance, adoption, legitimacy, guardianship, gifts, partitions and non-charitable trusts; *Wakafs* and the definition and regulation of charitable and religious endowments, institutions, trusts, charities and charitable institutions operating wholly within the State; Malay customs. Zakat, Fitrah and Baitulmal or similar Islamic religious revenue, mosques or any Islamic public places of worship, creation and punishment of offences by persons professing the religion of Islam against precepts of that religion, except in regard to matters included in the Federal List; the constitution, organisation and procedure of Syariah courts, which shall have jurisdiction only over persons professing the religion of Islam and in respect only of any of the matters included in this paragraph, but shall not have jurisdiction in respect of offences except in so far as conferred by federal law, the control of propagating doctrines and beliefs among persons professing

the religion of Islam; the determination of matters of Islamic law and doctrine and Malay custom."

4. The administration of Islam is a state and territory matter (and not a federal matter) and there are differences in the details of the roles played by the bodies in different states and territories. Within a state or territory, three bodies in particular are involved in the administration of Islam. These are the Syariah courts, the Council, and the Department. In the state of Selangor, for example, these bodies are respectively called the Mahkamah Syariah Selangor, Majlis Agama Islam Selangor, and Jabatan Agama Islam Selangor. Worth noting here are two federal bodies, neither of which has the power to enact law, but instead play advisory or coordinating roles: the Majlis Fatwa Kebangsaan (National Fatwa Council) issues *fatwas* that states and territories may then adopt and the Jabatan Kemajuan Islam Malaysia (Department of Islamic Development Malaysia), among other things, drafts laws and policies that states and territories may adopt, but also is in charge of *halal* (permissible) certification in Malaysia.

5. See Abdul K.S. (1998).

6. That is, the State List is a list that *empowers* the state to make law, and only after law is made does the Syariah court have jurisdiction.

5

ISLAMIST LAWYERS' VIEWS

I concentrate in this chapter on the views of some Islamist lawyers on the political and legal framework of Malaysia. I present first the views of Mohamed Ariff Yusof and Haji Sulaiman Abdullah. Their views relate more to political and ethnic interrelations and the rightful place of Islam in Malaysia. The second half of this chapter concerns the more narrowly legal arguments promulgated by the late professor of law in Singapore and Malaysia, Ahmad Ibrahim. Although he admits the Constitution to be secular, he develops a sophisticated (and arguably constitutionally sound) argument by which Islamic law could be given primacy over the Constitution and all other laws in Malaysia. The views, arguments, and sentiments examined in here are of the kind that activists must address in their defence of freedom of religion in Malaysia. Before moving on in Chapter 6 to a description of one civil society initiative instigated to mount such a defence, I examine Salbiah Ahmad's response to some of the arguments of Ahmad Ibrahim. She points out the important limitations of wholly legal challenges.

THE VIEWS OF MOHAMED ARIFF YUSOF AND HAJI SULAIMAN ABDULLAH

On Thursday 23 September 2004, I attended in Kuala Lumpur a Harvard Club colloquium titled "Islam Today: Themes and Issues". I understood that many of those in attendance were Harvard graduates, while others had received invitations. I belonged to the latter group. The two speakers for the evening were both members of the Malaysian Bar and advocates for the replacement of civil law with Syariah law. They both spoke with apparent candour and shared their views and opinions on current trends pertaining to Islam politically, socially, and legally.

Mohamed Ariff Yusof

The first speaker at the colloquium, Mohamed, was keen to stress to his largely non-Muslim audience that Islam's image as a religion of terrorism did not reflect Islam as it really was. No Muslim would condone the attacks on the Twin Towers in New York nor any attacks on innocent people. He deplored the biased portrayal of Islam in the American media which he described as full of fear and hate and he assured his audience that "there is nothing to fear from Islam". He asked his audience to keep an open mind to the ideas coming from what he described as the "Islamist movement".

Mohamed complained that, owing to outcry from non-Muslims in Malaysia, Islamists were not being given the opportunity to discuss issues such as Malaysia as an Islamic state, Hudud laws, or apostasy. He claimed Malaysia was not straightforwardly secular because Islam as the religion of the federation as stated in Article 3 must be regarded as having ramifications. Judges over the years have recognized the important place that Islam has in Malaysia. He cited a decision which deemed it unconstitutional to prohibit male students from wearing the Muslim turban. "True, the Constitution as it stands is a secular Constitution. But adjustments were made in the process of Constitution making. When the Reid Commission first drafted the Constitution they omitted all reference to Islam." It was because of the protests of the Sultans and opposition parties that Islam is the religion of the federation "and the repercussions are still felt today".

Mohamed went on to say,

> We've always argued as part of the Islamic movement that it is part of the freedom of religion provision in the Constitution that *muftis* should be allowed to articulate [their views] and if they get command of the majority of support through democratic means, to implement what they are arguing for as Muslims.

Later, in response to a question, he went on to say that Muslims refer to Islam as "*adeen*, as a way of life", and that to live as Muslims do in other countries where they are minorities is unacceptable in Malaysia where Muslims are a sizeable majority. "It is simply unIslamic. ... To a lot of

Muslims this cannot be the case. We cannot be subjected to an overriding civil court jurisdiction, particularly in Malaysia."

Haji Sulaiman Abdullah

The second speaker was Sulaiman who represented the counsel for the Majlis Agama Islam Wilayah Persekutuan in Lina Joy's appeal (see Chapter 4). He began by pointing out that his brother was a Harvard graduate and that, on completing his education, his brother brought back drinking glasses that were etched with the word "*veritas*". One's understanding of *veritas* — truth — however, is highly dependent on one's historical perspective he said. With this in mind, he said that he wished to outline three issues about which there are differing perceptions of truth: Turkey, Palestine, and the story of Maria Hertogh (of which I visit only the first and last, so little did he touch on Palestine).

Most extensively, Sulaiman spoke about Turkey. "The non-Muslim perception of Turkey has always been that Turkey was such a backward place until this glorious modernizer, Kemal Atatürk, came along, changed the whole face of Turkey and made it such a progressive modern nation and controlled Islam. ... In 1924 the *Kilafah*, or the Caliphate, which was always there as a symbol of Muslim unity, was abolished by Kemal Atatürk." Atatürk introduced secularism and, whereas the non-Muslim perception is that secularism is good, the Muslim perception is that secularism is anti-Islamic.

Atatürk also introduced the "Hat Law". "In order for Turkey to be modern," Sulaiman went on, Atatürk ruled that "Turkish men would not wear the fez any longer. They had to wear a cap with a brim. Ostensible reason: everybody in Europe wears a cap with a brim. Real reason: if you wear a cap with a brim, you cannot pray because your forehead will not be able to touch the ground." But "Islam being Islam", the Turkish men turned the cap around and were thus able to pray and obey the Hat Law.

Sulaiman related how, when he was in Turkey, he was taken to a war museum. On that day there was a military band playing. They initially played various tunes that enthused neither the band nor the audience. However, when they later played Ottoman army music, "suddenly they were vigorous, they were stamping their feet. You could see that they really *felt* the music they were performing". Sulaiman reported that he turned to his guide to ask what they were singing. The guide replied, "We are fighting in the way of Allah. We are fighting for Islam". Sulaiman went on, "those illiterate Turkish soldiers, with their heads scraped bare ... they still had sufficient Islam.

Bear in mind all the oppression, all the contra-Islam. Still Islam existed in their hearts. ... So bear in mind," he told if not warned the audience, "you can control Islam, you can make it difficult, but all you do is to strengthen Islam in people's hearts".

The third issue Sulaiman addressed was that of Maria Hertogh. He described this case from the early 1950s. The case involved, as Sulaiman described it,

> a little girl who was looked after by Muslims, became a Muslim, was married to a Muslim, and then her Dutch parents came back and claimed her and an English judge in Singapore reinvented the law in order to give her back to her Christian parents. And there was a picture in the newspapers of this little girl before a statue of the Virgin Mary or Jesus Christ and immediately Muslim tempers flared across Singapore and there were tremendous riots. The non-Islamic perception is that you really can't trust these Muslims. They just go wonky at the slightest excuse. ... This is the typical Lee Kuan Yew response. We have to control the Muslims to prevent Maria Hertogh from happening again. The Muslim response would be: whenever we feel that our religion is in danger, whenever we feel that people are being taken away from us by force, be it the issues of *murtad* or apostasy that Ariff was mentioning just now, immediately, because of the deep feelings of Islam, this will come up, will surface, and be very strong.

Reflections on the Evening

After the colloquium, I was given a ride to a train station by two Catholic Fathers who had also attended the evening. Both were familiar with the ideas of Islamists and, indeed, one had a number of acquaintances in PAS. I asked them during the trip how they felt. Both said that they had heard Islamists before, but that was the first time they had ever come away from a presentation feeling so unsettled.

I gathered that their unease stemmed from Sulaiman's comments. Whereas Mohamed averred that non-Muslims had nothing to fear from Islam, Sulaiman came across differently. His portrayal of Muslims in his accounts of Turkey, and especially in the Maria Hertogh affair, appeared to be evident warnings. Sulaiman suggested in the latter example that the reactions of the Muslims in Singapore would recur should Malaysians advocate too strongly for Muslims to apostatize legally. It should be noted here that the case of Maria Hertogh received a great deal of attention at the time, including from overseas. It was read by many Muslims as a Christian attack on Islam. In the 1950s court cases in Singapore, Maria Hertogh's

Dutch parents eventually won custody from her adopted Muslim Indonesian mother. Following this, there were three days of rioting in Singapore, mainly by ethnic Malays. As a result of these riots eighteen people were killed (see Hughes 1980).

In 2007 Sulaiman made a similar reference to violence in a magazine interview in response to a question regarding an angry gathering of Malay-Muslims at a church which, according to a widely circulated SMS, was helping Muslims to convert to Christianity.

> Let me put it this way. The traditional Malay is a very reserved kind of person. Normally, even when their rights are affected, they do not react because it is *tak sopan* [not polite]. But there is the danger of bottling that up and ultimately having amok. ... Insofar as the SMS is concerned, you have to realise that murtad — apostasy — is one of the most deadly sins in Islam and it would behove the religious authorities to take a very strong view of that. If there's any possibility of it occurring, they must act and they must be seen to act. And they must tell the community to act (in Tan J. 2007, p. 45; emphasis original, parentheses mine).

Allusions to the communal riots and to *amok*, and suggesting that the same feelings that gave rise to them would and should arise again if Malaysians were to defend the rights of Muslims to convert out of Islam would be a reasonable cause for concern for many liberal constitutionalists. The allusions made by Sulaiman are by no means confined to him as I described in Chapter 2. However, suffice it to say that its effect at the Harvard Colloquium was to intimidate non-Muslims from trespassing into the political territory that he regarded as belonging to Muslims.

Direct public engagement and threats of social instability are by no means the only way by which Islamists advance their agenda. Like liberal constitutionalists, they also advance interpretations of legal documents, such as the Constitution. One prominent figure in Malaysian law is the late Ahmad Mohamed Ibrahim (1916–99). It is to his legal arguments for the advancements of Syariah law in Malaysia that I now turn.

AHMAD MOHAMED IBRAHIM

Ahmad was active as a lawyer as well as a teacher and drafter of Islamic law in Singapore and Malaysia. He was, incidentally, counsel for Maria Hertogh's adopted mother (Hooker 1986, p. 5). In 1968 he migrated from Singapore to Malaysia and became involved in the establishment of the Faculty of Law at Universiti Malaya and later the International Islamic University of Malaysia where he became the Head of the Law School (Adabi 1986, pp. 21–22). According to Al-Mansor Adabi, during the 1970s Ahmad called for the improvement and upgrading of the administration of Islamic law in Malaysia and called for the recognition of Islamic law as the law of the land for Muslims in Malaysia. Adabi writes,

> When he first spoke about these matters in the 1970s, they appeared strange and outlandish, coming especially from a western educated lawyer, but it speaks a great deal for the influence of Ahmad Ibrahim as a teacher and public speaker that these matters have come to be generally accepted today (ibid., pp. 21–22).

Judges frequently quote Ahmad in their judgements and thus it is with good reason that I examine Ahmad's arguments for the Islamizing of Malaysian law.

In his essay "The Principles of an Islamic Constitution and the Constitution of Malaysia: A Comparative Analysis" (in Ahmad 2000), Ahmad acknowledges that the Constitution was not drafted as an Islamic constitution and that it is regarded by many, including Malaysia's first Prime Minister Tunku Abdul Rahman, as a secular constitution (ibid., pp. 395, 400; cf. Moten 2003, p. 2). He asks rhetorically, "What then is the remedy?"

Ahmad endeavours to locate legitimacy for the existence of Islamic law in Malaysia in two ways. First, he concedes that the definition of "Law" in Article 160 of the Constitution[1] does not recognize Islamic law and so it may be argued that Islamic law is not recognized in Malaysia. However, he writes that the definition "uses the term 'includes' and so can be extended to embrace the Islamic Law" (ibid., p. 398). He goes on to point out that Islamic law is recognized in the State List of the Ninth Schedule of the Constitution.

The matters enumerated in the State List on which the states can legislate in relation to Islam are largely limited to personal and family law. Ahmad then offers three approaches by which the jurisdiction of Islamic law can be expanded. One of these is to argue that Article 3 entitles Muslims "to lead their way of life according to the teachings of Islam" and that "[i]f [Muslims] wish to follow the Islamic Law rather than the Common Law, they should be allowed to do so" (ibid., p. 396). This reading of Article 3 would give it greater effect than that spelt out in the decision handed down in *Che Omar bin Che Soh* in which Islam's relationship with Malaysia was decided as being purely ceremonial.

A second method that Ahmad suggests (like Mohamed did at the Harvard Colloquium) is constitutional change or amendment through the mobilization of political power. Ahmad writes,

If Muslims want to make the Constitution more in line with Islam, they have to ensure that they will be in a position to amend it, that is, by registering as voters and electing representatives who can have a two-thirds majority in the Houses of Parliament for such amendments to be adopted (ibid., p. 400).

He immediately adds, "For this purpose, we must strive to be united so that we can better serve the cause of our people, our religion and our country." The last of Ahmad's suggestions that I shall examine is the most sophisticated and strictly legal. He writes,

It may be argued that Article 4 of the Federal Constitution makes the Constitution the supreme law of the country. Let us however read Article 4 in a positive manner. Article 4(1) reads:-

This Constitution is the supreme law of the Federation and any law passed after Merdeka Day [Independence Day] which is inconsistent with this constitution shall to the extent of the inconsistency, be void.

It should be argued that this refers only to the written law. The Constitution is the supreme law of the Federation. Even so, it only affects the validity of any law passed after Merdeka Day. There is a special position for pre-Merdeka laws which are not rendered invalid by inconsistency with the Constitution but have to be modified. The Privy Council in a case from Singapore has decided that the Constitution is subject to the principles of the Common Law and may be limited by it. In the context of Malaysia it can be argued that the Constitution cannot affect the validity of the Shariah which is non-written and is certainly not passed after Merdeka Day, although it may affect the legislation in relation to the administration of Islamic Law (ibid., p. 397).

To make sense of Ahmad's contention, one requires a clear understanding of the terms "Syariah Law" (or just "Syariah"), "Islamic Law", "statutory law", and "*fiqh*".

One can regard Syariah law, or the Syariah — which in Arabic translates as the path to the watering hole or the spring itself (Newby 2002, p. 193) — as an expansive body of knowledge and methodologies that jurists use in order to come to a judgement on a particular issue. Gordon Newby defines Syariah as referring to

God's law in its divine and revealed sense. This is related to fiqh, which is the human process of understanding and implementing the law. Commentators have argued that the aggregate of all the sources by which we know God's law is but a small part of shari'ah, which, like God, is unknowable and must be accepted (2002, p. 193).

Islamic law on the other hand may be regarded as statutes produced by legislation within the context of a modern State that has some relationship with Islam or Syariah law. "Syariah law" and "Islamic law" are very often used interchangeably. Affirming the difference, however, Aharon Layish stresses that codification of the Syariah (since the middle of the nineteenth century) has "brought about the transformation of the *shari'a* from 'jurists' law,' that is, a law created by independent legal experts, to 'statutory law,' in other words, a law promulgated by a national-territorial legislature" (Layish 2004, p. 86). Layish also points out that "*shari'a* is not a positive law". Instead, "it is first and foremost a system of religious ethical commandments and precepts some of which were translated over the years into legal terms with specified sanctions (as in the case of usury)" (ibid., p. 87). Indeed, Layish considers statutory Islamic law as so at odds with Syariah law that he states, "legislative authority is alien to Islam" (ibid., p. 88).

By understanding the unwritten and always-existing nature of Syariah law as it is conceived by many Muslims, we can see why Ahmad considers it as "certainly not passed after Merdeka Day" and possibly among those laws that may legally contradict the Constitution. Thus, it seems that Ahmad conceives of specific Islamic law *legislation* as being somehow a *manifestation* of pre-existing Syariah law.

RESPONDING TO ISLAMIST INTERPRETATIONS AND AGENDAS

It must be noted, however, that throughout his writing, Ahmad is imprecise in his usage of the terms "Syariah (Law)" and "Islamic Law". According to Salbiah Ahmad, a former student of Ahmad Ibrahim's, this imprecision may well be deliberate. She tells me that in her own writing, she uses three terms, "Syariah", "Islamic Law", and "*fiqh*", and defines them precisely (in the manner I outlined above). I asked her, "But surely Ahmad Ibrahim must know that 'Syariah' is a vague term?" "Yes", Salbiah told me,

> but he wants to get his foot in the door. You see, for instance, I read a newspaper survey a while ago that reported that if you ask Muslims whether they want the Syariah, they'll say 'yes'. If you then ask, 'do you want Hudud?' they'll say 'yes' again. But then if you tell them that Hudud means cutting off hands and stoning, they don't want it anymore.

She went on to say, "So what Islamists are doing is getting their foot in the door, without defining it, and letting it grow from there."

Salbiah is critical of Ahmad's contention that Syariah law is superior to the Constitution, in that it can limit it. Likewise is she critical of his contention that the Constitution can be read as recognizing Syariah law. She said,

> If the Constitution recognized parallel systems of Islamic law and civil law, or that it recognized the supremacy of Islamic law, it would be spelled out *in bold*. That is how a Constitution works. The Tunku [Abdul Rahman, Malaysia's first Prime Minister], during Dr Mahathir's Islamization drive, denounced Mahathir's Islamization project, saying that it was never intended in the Constitution. Malaysia was meant to be secular.

Even though historical interpretations may be adduced in support of Malaysia as a secular state and even though people may challenge Islamic interpretations of Malaysia's law and Constitution, Salbiah makes a point that cannot be overlooked in any examination of the issues addressed here.

> A legal challenge [to Islamic interpretations of the Constitution] is one way of working towards change but legal challenges will not survive the wider political and social forces that will bring to bear on it. Any legal challenge will have to run in tandem with wider societal strategies in the political and socio-cultural spheres (Salbiah 2003, p. 88).

The idea that legal strategies alone were insufficient was evident to a number of the liberal constitutionalists with whom I spoke in Malaysia. In recognition of this fact, in 2004, a coalition of NGOs and individuals formed to mobilize and create political support for a liberal reading of religious freedom in Article 11. This coalition called itself *Article 11*. I shall now turn away from some of the work that has taken place more squarely within the legal framework, to that which involves the social activism necessary to defend a liberal interpretation of the Constitution.

Notes

1. According to Article 160, "'Law' includes written law, the common law in so far as it is in operation in the Federation or any part thereof, and any custom or usage having the force of law in the Federation or any part thereof."

6

SOCIAL ACTIVISM AND THE
ARTICLE 11 COALITION

At the end of the previous chapter, some of the limitations for liberal constitutionalists of wholly legal approaches were recognized. In this chapter I
examine an example of social activism in response to the failure of legal
challenges to Islamically founded restrictions on freedom of religion. I
begin by describing the formation of a coalition of lawyers and activists
called *Article 11*. I then indicate the efficacy of extralegal activism by briefly
describing a particular case on which they focussed public attention.

ARTICLE 11

On 26 June 2004, a coalition of more than ten NGOs conducted a day-long
public forum in the auditorium of the Malaysian Bar Council. This coalition
was named *Article 11*[1] after the article in the Constitution that articulates
freedom of religion. The forum drew an audience of some two hundred
people made up of lawyers, interested lay people, and social activists.

Article 11 coalition members had been concerned with the erosion of
constitutionally enshrined fundamental liberties. This erosion is the result of
the increase in the social and political legitimacy of Islam. The influence of
Islam in civil law and the deference of the civil courts to the Syariah courts
on some matters has adversely affected the rights of those who belong to
religions other than Islam, of those who are Muslim but do not wish to

follow State sanctioned interpretations of Islam, and, as we shall see, also of women, both Muslim and non-Muslim. The coalition was formed to organize social and political activism when lawyers and activists realized that the erosion of liberties brought about by Islamization was not a problem that could be remedied by action within the courtroom alone. It was a socio-political problem that could only be countervailed if accompanied by socio-political engagement. As put by Malik Imtiaz Sarwar, who spoke at this forum,

> There is no benefit to be gained now ... in waiting for some magic miracle to occur in the courts. ... The courts are merely, in their minds, correctly reflecting political will as they understand it. ... I think the issue is not a legal one at all. It is a socio-political consideration.

Article 11 is composed of various NGOs, only some of which have religious orientations.[2] Some are women's NGOs who are concerned because Islamic law and the Islamist movement contain elements that discriminate against women (see also Zainah 2005, pp. 127–29). The case which precipitated the formation of *Article 11* involved the case of a non-Muslim woman whose children were converted to Islam without her consent and who, as a result, risked losing custody of them.

Many in Malaysia saw this case as emblematic of Syariah law's unwarranted intrusion into the lives of non-Muslims, of its poor regard for women's rights, and the conflict into which it can come with civil law and the Constitution. It thus became the focus of a concerted effort by the *Article 11* coalition to pressure the Court of Appeal to grant the mother custody of her children and a say in deciding their religion. By briefly presenting the facts of the case below, I will be able to portray the quandary in which the mother of these children found herself and also to portray the impact that *Article 11* had on the decision of the judge in the appeal hearing.

The Case of Shamala Sathiyaseelan

In 1998 Ms Shamala Sathiyaseelan and Dr Jeyaganesh Mogarajah were married according to Hindu rites and subsequently had two boys. In 2002 Dr Jeyaganesh converted to Islam after which he took the name Dr Muhammad Ridzan Mogarajah. Dr Jeyaganesh meanwhile converted his two children to Islam without their mother's consent. While Ms Sathiyaseelan and Dr Muhammad remained married, they became estranged. In late 2002 both parents applied for custody of the children, although Ms Sathiyaseelan applied to the High Court while Dr Muhammad applied to the Syariah

Court (in the state of Selangor). Dr Muhammad was made to attend the High Court in January 2003 but applied for and received an adjournment. He neglected at this time to inform the High Court of his own application for custody in the Syariah court. In February 2003 Ms Sathiyaseelan was served an order to attend the Syariah court which she ignored on the grounds that, as a Hindu, she had no standing there. The Syariah court then issued a warrant for the arrest of Ms Sathiyaseelan for failure to attend the hearing. In April 2003 the High Court stayed this warrant and gave Ms Sathiyaseelan interim custody of her children. In May 2003 Ms Sathiyaseelan filed (in the civil courts) for an order against her husband for failing to comply with the interim order and her husband then filed for divorce (in the Syariah courts). Ms Sathiyaseelan was again summoned to the Syariah court, this time about the divorce and custody of the children. She did not attend.

On 13 April 2004 and in accord with the Attorney-General's Chambers' recommendations, the High Court dismissed Ms Sathiyaseelan's application for an annulment of the conversion to Islam of her children on the grounds that only the Syariah courts have the competency and the expertise to determine the religion of the children. Judge Faiza also acknowledged, however, that Ms Sathiyaseelan had no *locus standi* to seek relief in the Syariah court and was thus being asked to apply to a court in which she (as a non-Muslim) had no legal standing. He thus recommended that Ms Sathiyaseelan seek assistance from the Majlis Agama Islam Selangor (Islamic Council of Selangor) or from Parliament.

Issues Arising from Ms Sathiyaseelan's Case

In the view of the *Article 11* coalition, the issues apparent in this case are becoming increasingly common. Although *Article 11* is concerned with issues of freedom of religion per se, Ms Sathiyaseelan's case was used to highlight the gendered aspect of those issues.

Meera Samanther of the Women's Aid Organisation, and Pushpa Ratnam, the legal advisor of the All Women's Action Society of Malaysia, respectively presented a summary of Ms Sathiyaseelan's story and an outline of the issues that arose from it. The first of these issues regarded the jurisdiction of the civil court in matters pertaining to conversion to and from Islam. In Ms Sathiyaseelan's case, the High Court was unwilling to make any ruling with regard to the official religion of the two young children. The civil court decided that jurisdiction for this matter lay with the Syariah courts.

The second issue related to the legal impact of the husband's conversion to Islam and its negative repercussions on his wife. In *Article 11's* view the findings of the court contradicted Article 8 of the Constitution which guarantees that citizens, regardless of sex or religion, will be treated equally. It also contradicted Section 5 of the Guardianship of Infants Act which states that both the mother and father of an infant have equal rights in determining such matters as education, health, social interaction, and religion. The 13 April 2004 decision, according to Ratnam, "is akin to slamming the door shut on her rights as a mother".

Ratnam went on to tell the audience at the forum that many women in situations similar to Ms Sathiyaseelan's have sought the help of the women's organizations in *Article 11*. In these cases, "a woman stands to lose custody and guardianship of her children when the husband converts to Islam". To prevent this, asserted Ratnam, recognition of equal rights to guardianship must prevail.

Given that conversion of one's religion to Islam entails legal impacts that affect a wife, Ratnam suggested that it is only right that the authorities overseeing the conversion inform the spouse of the conversion. This is because there are numerous legal impacts on the spouse in such a case. These include the dispensation of estates upon death. More significantly, however, is that although the wife has no choice but to accept the conversion of her husband's religion to Islam (as per his right as enshrined in Article 11), current law demands that the wife choose to either convert her religion to Islam or file for divorce. A common reason given for this is that entry of a man into Islam permits polygamous marriages which are not permitted to non-Muslims. Ratnam doubted that forcing a woman to choose between divorce or conversion to Islam was fair.

A third issue relates to the fact that there was no legal remedy available to Ms Sathiyaseelan. Although Judge Faiza stated that the civil court's custody order was not overridden by the custody order from the Syariah court, and although he declared that the arrest warrant issued by the Syariah court for Ms Sathiyaseelan was unconstitutional, he nevertheless suggested to Ms Sathiyaseelan that she have the Majlis Agama Islam Selangor bring the matter to the Syariah court, or that Parliament be waited upon for a change in legislation. Neither leave Ms Sathiyaseelan, as a non-Muslim, with any active recourse or options. We may thus observe that Ms Sathiyaseelan has been forced into a lacunae where no law applies.

Restrictions within Islam

Two other areas of concern regarding the practice of freedom of religion in Malaysia were addressed at this seminar. The first of these related to restrictions on the rights of Muslims to practise Islam in a manner not in accord with that sanctioned by the State. The second related to restrictions that adversely affect the ability of non-Muslims to engage in religious activities.

At the seminar, Mrs Kamariah Ali related to the audience her experiences after being charged in 1992 for practising Islam in a manner inconsistent with official Islamic teachings. She faced this charge with three others: Mr Daud Mamat, Mr Mad Yacob Ismail, and her late husband, Mr Mohamad Ya. The four were convicted of the said offence by the Syariah High Court of Kelantan and jailed for between two and five years. In 1996 their appeal against the conviction was rejected, but their sentences were altered. They were then required to report every month to the Syariah court judge's office to repent. However, they stopped reporting after twice being told that their repentance classes were not ready.

In 1998 all four renounced Islam by way of statutory declarations. They were subsequently charged with attempting to leave Islam and were jailed for contempt. Over the course of the next two years, applications to the High Court and the Court of Appeal were made and subsequently dismissed. In late 2002 the four were released from prison after serving two-thirds of their sentences.

Because of the civil courts' willingness to confer away jurisdiction on matters pertaining to Islam, organizers of the forum were concerned that Islamic law is gaining greater legal weight than the Constitution. At the forum, Haris bin Mohamed Ibrahim said of the civil court judges who would not clarify the religious status of the people in Mrs Kamariah's and Ms Sathiyaseelan's cases, that they have

> abdicated in their duty ... by the simple mechanism ... of finding jurisdiction in some other court, which 'til this day cannot be justified by written law. ... To my mind, that is nothing short of an abdication of their duty owed to the citizenry.

However, of concern to *Article 11* is not only that people who are regarded by State apparatuses as Muslims are having various freedoms curtailed, but unambiguously non-Muslim citizens and religious organizations face impediments to the practice of their religion on ostensibly Islamic grounds.

Freedom of Religion for Non-Muslims

At the *Article 11* forum, Hacharan Singh, the then President of the Malaysian Consultative Council of Buddhism, Christianity, Hinduism and

Sikhism, described some of the restrictions that are placed on non-Muslims. Singh gave an account of a woman who had converted her religion to Islam merely in order to marry a Muslim man. The marriage fell through, however, and she was then left as a Muslim with barely any knowledge about or inclination towards Islam. He emphasized that there were many others in similar situations to this woman and that these were not projected or hypothetical fears, but current and real.

Singh also informed the audience that there are certain words, such as "Allah", that are forbidden to be used by non-Muslims in certain circumstances on the grounds that the words are for use by Muslims only. However, many of these words occur in other religions as well. The word Allah, said Singh, was used by the Sikhs' Guru Nani and occurs in the Sikh's depositions from God (see also Kairos 2004, pp. 51–55). Singh stressed that such restrictions did not exist prior to independence.

He also explained that in some areas of Malaysia, there are restrictions on the architectural appearance of certain religious buildings. Sikh temples (*gurdwara*) around the world have domes. According to Singh, however, in some places, authorities say that temples should not have domes because Muslims may mistake them for mosques. Singh went on to note that this restriction has been enforced even though there was no law to that effect. He went on to note that before a religious building can be built, it must be proved that there are five thousand people of the given faith in a given area. Singh related that there had been no such "catchment area" in the past. Furthermore, he went on to say, this requirement is very difficult for Sikhs to meet given their relatively low numbers.

The causes of these restrictions and impositions on non-Muslims were owing, according to Singh, to political pressures. The declaration that Malaysia was an Islamic state allowed civil servants and law-makers to create and enforce laws that impinged on the rights of non-Muslims. However, he went on, people allow it to happen because Muslims are the majority of the population. "But how much [of a] majority?" he went on to ask.

> It is not ninety-eight or ninety-nine per cent. It is maybe sixty-forty! ... But does that make Malaysia an Islamic state? But in law it isn't there. There's no firm legal or factual definition of what is an Islamic state. ... If there is an Islamic state, there is an automatic disability on a non-Muslim. In a real Islamic state a non-Muslim cannot be an equal citizen to a Muslim.

Following the presentations of the various speakers at this forum, audience members were invited to express their views on the issues raised.

Most of the remarks and questions pertained to a handful of concerns. The principal of these related to equality between the religions. In various ways and drawing on different examples, speakers expressed their desire for their country to treat members of all religions equally. One woman, for example, asserted that if the government was to have a department for Islamic affairs it should also have one for Buddhist, Christian, and Hindu affairs.

Another recurring concern was over Mahathir's announcement in 2001 that Malaysia is an Islamic state. For many that statement was not innocuous. It gave legitimacy to the Islamist movement and expanded its boundaries. This was a concern because even before the pronouncement many non-Muslims had already felt like second-class citizens or *dhimmi* (people living under Muslim rule who are subject to restrictions and taxes not applied to Muslims; see Martinez 2004, p. 35).

The Frog in the Water and Changing the Socio-Political Climate

One audience member during the question-and-answer session at the Harvard Colloquium (discussed in Chapter 4), referring to the Islamization of Malaysia, said gravely, "this is not a funny issue. It goes to the heart of every Malaysian." Malik, at the *Article 11* forum, framing the issue within the concept of the social contract in Malaysia, asked, "Are we or are we not an Islamic state? At the heart of the social contract discussion is that question in the context of the problems we are hoping to address today."

The allusion to the heart is indicative of the centrality and vitalness of the issue of the Islamic identity of Malaysia. A metaphor of a frog in water that was used by lawyer Leonard Teoh at the forum indicates its pervasiveness and almost physiological importance.

> I know a lot of people who say to themselves, "If I can drink, if I can eat pork, if I can gamble, if I can pray in my church or temple or follow my Buddhist beliefs, what's wrong with that? Let things be." But slowly it is creeping up on us. As somebody put it, "PAS has put the frog into the pot of hot boiling water. UMNO put the frog in the pot and then boiled the water." Either way we're going to get burned.

The metaphor of the frog in water, at risk of being either instantly or gradually boiled, has resonance with that of the stream used by the anthropologist Michael Jackson in speaking of the person who has experienced trauma or is in shock. Of relevance is that the "world of alterity, with which one had worked out a *modus vivendi*, suddenly becomes a threat, an enemy, a contagion" (2002, pp. 71–72). While the metaphor is used around the world, its meaning for those at the *Article 11* forum was localized. In the case of the Malaysians at the *Article 11* forum, the relationship that they had with Islam, an alterity for many, was changing. Previously outside the bounds or incidental to their lives, Islam was permeating their world. The changes that were being wrought — the attrition of their *modus vivendi*, the loss of efficacy they experience as lawyers and activists, the transformation of the framework of their world — was putting their worlds at as much risk as the life of the frog in the water. In the same way as water about to boil threatened the frog, Islamization and the Islamic state threatened their belonging, the foundation of their interpersonal relations, and the framework of their lives. The resultant reduction of efficacy is true not only for ordinary people, but also for NGOs and lawyers who advocate for justice and fairness as they understand it. Their usual tools and discourses are losing effectiveness as the environment, indeed the social and political framework, in which they function changes.

However, in spite of the exhortations by the presenters at the seminar that a public reaction is necessary to reverse the legal and political trends that were outlined, one audience member suggested to the panel that their problem be tackled by "going back to the courts". Haris replied to this by saying,

> Our concern is this: unless you have running parallel with matters that are being filed in court the sentiment of the public being registered and registered loudly, so that the courts must take notice ... every other matter that we file becomes a further nail in the coffin. Because every time we file a matter in court, time and again, the judges are saying, "No jurisdiction. Jurisdiction rests with the Syariah Court." Now, quite honestly, I have several other matters in my office of a similar nature with [Mrs] Kamariah Ali's, but I dare not file these matters in court because I am giving the judges ammunition to shut the coffin forever. Now, do we have hope? I have hope — if the public sees the problem and from today chooses to no longer remain silent. Without that backing I will personally continue to tell my clients that the time is not right. And I think it's wrong. It is wrong to take a position of "the time is not right", because it is never a right time. [Mrs] Kamariah and the three others served time. How do we tell them that "it is not expedient at this time to pursue this issue?" I think none of us has the moral right to take that position ... [Legal challenges] must move in tandem with a public outcry.

Haris's statement that every other matter that he files in court risks shutting the coffin forever refers to the legal weight of judicial precedent on future cases of this nature. If every legal angle is explored in a climate hostile to religious freedom, then precedent will preclude favourable decisions in spite of a more favourable climate which may possibly prevail in the future.

The Fruits of Activism

On 20 July 2004 the court heard the application of Ms Sathiyaseelan (*in absentia*) for custody, care, and control of the children. Custody was awarded to the mother and fortnightly access granted to the father. Dr Muhammad was also instructed to pay 20 per cent of his gross income as maintenance until they reached twenty-one years of age or, should his children cease to be Muslims, until they reached eighteen years of age. However, the judge inserted a caveat. Judge Faiza ruled that the mother would lose custody of the children if she influenced her children's religion (which was, in effect, assumed by the Judge to be Islam) by, for example, teaching them about Hinduism or by making them eat pork.

Those members of the *Article 11* coalition to whom I spoke outside of the forum described above, as well as other interested observers, all agreed that the decision was unworkable. Indeed, one woman who observed the judge handing down his decision said that he seemed fed up with the case and the attention that it was receiving. She went on to say that she thought he delivered his decision with the assumption that it would move directly to appeal. However unworkable it may be, the result did appear to demonstrate the efficacy of the accompanying activism. Throughout the hearing, various NGOs engaged the media and turned out in evident support of Ms Sathiyaseelan. Most agreed that without this activism the decision would have followed the trend seen in other similar cases and been more unfavourable to Ms Sathiyaseelan. The court would have probably decided that custody and the religion of the children would have to be entirely decided in the Syariah courts. Her case would certainly have gone against her there.

ARTICLE 11 BROUGHT TO A HALT

In 2006 members of *Article 11* began a "road show" of similar forums in different states. The first two states were Selangor and Melaka. In the former, more than 800 people attended the forum at which discussants affirmed that the Constitution should be regarded as the supreme law of Malaysia. An open letter signed by 450 attendees expressed concern over the civil court judges' declinations on ruling on cases that involved Islamic law, and which therefore left many litigants without legal remedy (Theophilus 2006*a*). Zaitun "Toni" Kasim, speaking about a forum held in March 2006, noted the increasing willingness of people to discuss issues such as freedom of religion. Furthermore, she observed, "The fact that all these people are here on a Sunday morning and stayed on till the end is very telling of the lack of discussion on the fundamental issues of freedom and rights. We need more space for dialogue" (quoted in ibid.).

However, the attempt by *Article 11* to mobilize support and to publicly discuss issues relating to the impact of Islam on non-Muslims and Muslims alike was interrupted in May 2006. Over 100 Muslim demonstrators gathered in protest outside the hotel in Penang in which the *Article 11* forum was being conducted. One placard, for example, proclaimed, "*Undang-undang Allah mengatasi hak asasi manusia*" (Allah's laws prevail over human rights). When some protestors "tried to storm the hotel" the police asked the organizers to wrap up the forum. One of the speakers said that "[i]t is of grave concern that we should stop a legitimate discussion when the people outside were the ones who were turning unruly" (quoted in Theophilus 2006*b*). Emphasizing that the forum was an open space where both affirmations and criticisms of *Article 11*'s agenda could be expressed, Haris said, "If [the protestors] had their own point of view, they should have come in and voiced it out." He went on to affirm that "[w]e [*Article 11*] have never practised censorship. In fact, we allocated two hours for a question-and-answer session. They could have equally participated" (quoted in ibid.). A forum on the same topic held in 2008, which was organized not by *Article 11* but by the Malaysian Bar Council, shared the same fate of being curtailed owing to threats from Islamist protestors outside of the Malaysian Bar Council building in Kuala Lumpur (see Lee 2008*b*).

I should note that subsequent to the ill-fated *Article 11* forum in Penang, Prime Minister Abdullah Badawi announced a gag order on discussions of the Constitution, especially as it relates to freedom of religion. And indeed, at the fifth Malaysian Studies Conference which I attended in August 2006 in Malaysia, a panel on the topic of the Constitution and freedom of religion was cancelled in view of this directive. But as one reporter wrote, "Abdullah has seen enough — not from the hardliners, though, as one might expect, but from Article 11" (Gatsiounis 2006). On the same day and in the same paper that reported that the social science conference panel had been cancelled (see Husna 2006), it was also reported that a coalition of Muslim NGOs known as Pembela was to gather to discuss recent events. They also sought to oppose any liberal interpretations of the Constitution (in a manner unfavourable to Islam) and "to challenge Article 11 [of the Constitution], which it sees as a threat to Muslim rights" (*The Sun* 2006). And indeed, since then, a different but related coalition of Muslim NGOs submitted a memorandum to then Prime Minister Abdullah Badawi and to the Council of Rulers. This memorandum urged the Prime Minister "to act against those quarters who challenged [the position of Islam] and 'encourage aberrations' in Islamic beliefs". It also urged Parliament to "amend Article 11 pertaining to religious freedom in conformity with syariah laws and teachings" (Fauwaz 2006).

It is worth noting that the precipitant of *Article 11*'s 2006 road show was a pair of court rulings that appeared to give further and unprecedented power to the Syariah courts. Both involved the determination of the religion of two deceased individuals. Following the death of "Everest hero" and army commander M. Moorthy in December 2005, a dispute ensued over his religion. Former army colleagues and the Syariah court declared that Moorthy had converted to Islam prior to his death and so ought to be given a Muslim burial. His Hindu wife, however, maintains that she had no knowledge of the alleged conversion, that he was a Hindu and, as evidence of this, was on television some weeks before his death discussing the meaning of the Hindu festival of Deepavali. The first she is said to have heard of the alleged conversion was while her husband was in the coma that preceded his death. A colleague of his informed her and added that their child would be claimed by the state authorities as Muslim (Malaysiakini.com 2005*b*). In late December the High Court deferred to the Syariah court stating that, pursuant to Article 121(1a) (see Chapter 4), the High Court had no jurisdiction in matters pertaining to Islam. He was consequently buried as a Muslim (Malaysiakini.com 2005*c*).

The second and more worrying case for *Article 11* was that of Nyonya binte Tahir. Occurring only a few weeks after that of M. Moorthy's, this case, which was heard in the Syariah court, has been described as a landmark. In question was Tahir's religion at the time of her death. Although the Syariah court found that Nyonya binte Tahir, an elderly woman, was a Buddhist and not a Muslim when she died, the case was of concern to many *Article 11* members despite perhaps being an apparently positive result. At a meeting in January 2006, I heard consternation expressed over the fact that the woman's non-Muslim relatives had attended the Syariah court to give evidence and thus were taken as having standing there. Furthermore, the case was being hailed by various commentators, including then Prime Minister Abdullah, as evidence that non-Muslims could find justice in the Syariah courts. The case was said to have demonstrated the progressiveness of the Syariah courts and that non-Muslims should not assume that the Syariah court was automatically disadvantaging them.

This decision, which occurred in the wake of the outcry that followed the M. Moorthy case, was considered by many in and out of *Article 11* as an evidently political decision. It was perceived to have been handed down to quell non-Muslim fears that the political and legal systems of Malaysia were wholly biased towards Islam as the M. Moorthy case seemed to suggest. However, the first concern among those at the *Article 11* meeting was that the decision would be seen as an indication that non-Muslims could and would receive equitable treatment in the Syariah courts. Secondly and primarily, however, they were troubled by the precedent of non-Muslims acting as legitimate participants in the Syariah courts. The consensus was that, more usually, non-Muslims in the Syariah courts would be unlikely to be successful or have their testimonies taken as seriously as those of Muslims. The short-term gain of these non-Muslims in the Nyonya binte Tahir case was seen as portending an expansion of the Syariah courts' ambit which some members had been ardently opposing for years.

The need to have public debate about these decisions was identified at the January 2006 *Article 11* meeting. Also identified was the need to enable progressive Muslims to speak and be heard because, as one member noted, "We need to open the gateway for moderates to speak. My [Muslim] friends often ask me, 'Where do we go? How do I speak up?'"

The constriction of public space for discussion of issues relating to the impact of Islam in politics and people's lives is apparent in the social and political reactions to public forums about freedom of religion described above. It is also apparent in police enforcement — at the Penang forum mentioned above for example — and also in direct statements from Malay politicians (for example Badruddin Amiruldin's warning (described in Chapter 2) that the riots of 1969 could be repeated if Malay rights were challenged (for similar remarks from another minister see Puah 2006)). Coercion into silence over matters pertaining to Islam affects even elected members of Parliament. Opposition MP Theresa Kok was detained without trial under the ISA in September 2008 for allegedly requesting a mosque in her constituency to turn down the volume of the call to prayer. Such is the intolerance to interference of the call to prayer that proposals put forward by the Jabatan Kemajuan Islam Malaysia (JAKIM, or Department of Islamic Development Malaysia) suggested restricting all broadcasts of entertainment programmes during it. In response to these proposals, which also included the segregation of males and females at concerts, Malaysian academic and political commentator Farish Noor has suggested that "[t]he conquest of the nation's temporal-spatial terrain has thus begun" (2005). Noor goes on to note that

> [o]ur national identity and the common shared collective temporal-spatial framework upon which the nation is to be built is being carved up by the religious functionaries who seem to be driven only by their own communitarian exclusive concerns. Worst of all, these religious functionaries are in the pay of the Malaysian government and state, which means that their schemes are being financed by the ordinary Malaysian tax-payer! Is this the Malaysia that our founding fathers envisaged, or are we actually witnessing the nascent Balkanisation of our country? (ibid.)

Although Malaysia's cabinet decided to "hold off" on the proposals to restrict programming during the call to prayer, that they were suggested indicates the presence of Islamist individuals within government institutions such as JAKIM. Furthermore, as a headline in a Malaysian newspaper read at the time, the proposals may yet return; the proposals were "off — for now" (*New Straits Times* 2005).

CONSTITUTING THE PUBLIC SPHERE

But Islamization in Malaysia threatens to swap popular sovereignty with divine sovereignty, thus replacing the *kratos* (power) of the *demos* (people) with the *kratos* of the *theos* (god) (or more accurately perhaps, those with the right to interpret the will of the *theos*) (cf. Castoriadis 1997*b*, p. 340). "Democracy", writes Jeremy Waldron,

> requires that when there is disagreement in a society about a matter on which a common decision is needed, every man and woman in the society has the right to participate on equal terms in the resolution of that disagreement (2002, p. 52).

The legal and political development of Islam has given grounds for fears that any further enlargements of Islam's place in legal and political realms will see the considerations of Muslims — and in particular Islamic authorities — in decision-making expand while those of the general population, especially non-Muslims, contract. Not everyone will participate in the public realm equally, not even in principle. Activists and lawyers focus on and defend their understanding of the Constitution because it outlines the fundamental political and legal framework of Malaysia. Changes to the Constitution and to how it is interpreted will therefore lead to fundamental changes in the political and legal realms. Gianfranco Poggi notes that a further significant meaning of "constitution," still echoed in frequent uses of the term constitutional, lies in the assumption that contention about the direction of policy is both legitimate and productive, provided it is bound by the contendents' shared commitment to some "rules of the game" (1990, p. 56).

The issue of religious freedom crystallizes what is at stake more broadly, namely, the nature of the rules of game. *Article 11*'s ongoing activism (see Article11.org) attempts to defend (as they see it) the Constitution from change, or to reassert the rules agreed to by Malaysia's founders, as any diversion or development is likely to see the game being played on a more uneven field.

Ahmed T. el-Gaili has noted that "[t]he primary challenge to an Islamic state is that substantive Islamic law concerning non-Muslims, as developed by classical scholars, treats non-Muslims as subjects with inferior political, legal, and religious rights" (2004, p. 521). Given that the government-produced document mentioned in Chapter 3, *"Malaysia adalah sebuah negara Islam"* (Malaysia is an Islamic State), refers to non-Muslims as *dhimmi* (see Martinez 2004, p. 33), and that there are areas in which non-Muslim Malaysians are already treated as such (ibid., p. 35), these non-Muslims, as well as non-conforming Muslims, have understandable cause for concern. Authors have noted that the mechanism of democracy may be used by Islamists to either overthrow democracy (e.g., Zartman 2001, p. 243) or to dominate or tyrannize non-Muslims (el-Gaili 2004). El-Gaili regards it as critical that protections for minorities "be institutionalized, whether through permanent rights enshrined in a constitution or a bill of rights or through a variety of structural measures that affords minorities an increased voice" (ibid., p. 511).

However, the protective constitutional framework and judicial inter-vention for which el-Gaili argues are already extant in Malaysia but are, as the foregoing chapters have demonstrated, failing Malaysia's minorities. One might look instructively at Nigeria, another former British colony with a Muslim majority. Nigeria's Constitution appears far less ambiguous as to the legal and political place of Islam. It is explicit in forbidding the country's legislature and executive branches from advancing or sponsoring religion (Nmehielle 2004, p. 742). It also unambiguously affirms a citizen's "freedom of thought, conscience and religion, including freedom to change his religion or belief" (ibid., p. 743). And yet, in spite of this, many states have introduced Syariah law, including the Hudud laws, since 1999. We might also note that, like Malaysian Islamists, Nigerian Islamists argue that instituting Syariah law is demanded of them as Muslims (ibid., p. 738) and that it is really the reintroduction of a legal system that was displaced by English civil law (ibid., p. 739). Given that the Malaysian Constitution is more ambiguous as to the role of Islam than the Nigerian Constitution, that Malaysia could yet become further Islamized is a serious possibility.

Given the undeniable influence that Islam plays in Malaysia's social and political life, it has become increasingly important for progressive Muslims to work within the framework of Islam to advance progressive or liberal agendas. Contesting the exclusivist and conservative interpretations of Islam and policies from State sanctioned bodies seems increasingly important given that attempts not eminating from within Islamic discourses have so far produced mixed results in protecting the equality and rights of Muslim women, of non-conforming Muslims, and non-Muslims. This work is also personally important for Muslims who feel that their religion is being distorted by Islamists and politicians. Thus it is to the work of those who work within Islam in this way that I now turn.

Notes

1. Where "Article 11" is italicized, it refers to the above described coalition. Where it is not italicized, it refers to the article in Malaysia's Constitution.
2. The coalition consists of, The Joint Action Group (itself a coalition comprised of Sisters in Islam; Women's Aid Organisation; Women's Centre for Change, Penang; All Women Action Society of Malaysia; Women's Development Collective; Malaysian Trade Union Congress, Women's Section), Malaysian Consultative Council of Buddhism, Christianity, Hinduism and Sikhism, Catholic Lawyers' Society, INSAF, Malaysian Bar Council, Pure Life Society, Vivekananda Youth Group, Catholic Bishops' Conference, Council of Churches, and Suara Rakyat Malaysia.

7

QUESTIONING ORTHODOXIES, CRITICIZING ZEALOTRY

I begin this chapter by describing the views of the Muslim women's NGO, Sisters in Islam (SIS). This high-profile NGO undertakes advocacy work surrounding women's rights in Islam and conducts educational trainings, one of which I describe below.

Like many Malaysian Muslims, of concern to members of SIS is the apparent conflation of Arab culture with Islam. This is sometimes referred to in Malaysia as the Arabization of Islam. This conflation is often associated with a conservatism that appears to be becoming increasingly liable to enforcement by State apparatuses. In this chapter I recount a raid of a nightclub by the Jabatan Agama Islam Wilayah Persekutuan (Federal Territory Islamic Department). Finally I explore the responses to this incident from different quarters of Malaysian society.

GOING BEYOND THE QURAN

On 12 June 2004, Farid Esack, a South African activist and academic, gave a talk at the Malaysian AIDS Council in Kuala Lumpur. He suggested that a pandemic such as AIDS raises theological issues. One issue he raised was that Muslims are supposed to be silent about their sins. He recollected a *Hadith*, a report of a saying or deed of the Prophet Muhammad, which he prefaced by noting his wariness of *Hadith* because one could be found in support of almost any position one cared to take. This *Hadith* was to the effect that the Prophet attempted to ignore a man who voluntarily confessed to *zinna* (illicit sexual conduct) to him. Only after the man's insistence and his fourth confession did the Prophet enforce the relevant punishment.[1] But with AIDS, said Esack, the silence that appears to be encouraged in this *Hadith* through the example of the Prophet's apparent disinterest in this confession could lead to death.

Esack also raised the issue of sexuality in Islam. Muslims who oppose homosexuality frequently cite verses 11:77–83 from the Quran as the justification of their view. These verses recount the story of Lot in which Sodomites and Gomorrahans are destroyed because of, it is frequently held, the residents' homosexual behaviour. However, Esack recalled the images of sexually humiliated Iraqi prisoners from Abu Ghraib.[2] When he asked the audience whether they found the images sexually arousing, they responded that they did not. Esack suggested that although there was certainly sex in those images, our usual associations of tenderness, legitimacy, and connectivity with sex are what make it different to violence. Why is it then, he asked rhetorically, that it is sex that is seen in Lot's tale, and not barbarism and domination, as in the Abu Ghraib images?

By way of a parallel, Esack recalled another *Hadith* in which a man reports to the Prophet that his brother has a stomach ache. The Prophet tells the man to give the brother honey, which was revealed in the Quran to have healing qualities.[3] Twice more the man returns to report that the ache was unhealed and at last the Prophet is said to have said, "God has spoken the truth, your brother's stomach has lied."

Esack suggested that today there are various realities such as AIDS, gender discrimination, and violence to which Muslims are trying to apply the honey of the Quran but the honey is not working. Some, he suggested, argue that it is not the honey, but how it is being taken. One problem is that it is only the interpretations of the Muslim texts that are being questioned, not the source itself. "We need to move away from text fundamentalism", he said. The Quran and the Prophet are a part of a heritage, not the whole of it, and the Quran is like the railing on a staircase, not the destination itself.

"TRY USING THAT APPROACH IN ADVOCACY!"

I left the presentation by Esack at the Malaysian AIDS Council with Zaitun "Toni" Kasim. Toni was active in a number of NGOs in Malaysia including the Malaysian AIDS Council, Suara Rakyat Malaysia (The Malaysian

People's Voice), and particularly, SIS. SIS is a Malaysian NGO that has generated interest among scholars and researchers in academic fields (e.g., Bell 1999, p. 854; Foley 2004, pp. 61–63; Mohamad 2004; Nagata 1997, p. 143; Peletz 2006, pp. 251–54) as well as among fellow NGOs. SIS describes itself as "a group of Muslim professional women committed to promoting the rights of women within the framework of Islam". Their promotion of Muslim women's rights is "based on the principles of equality, justice and freedom enjoined by the Qur'an as made evident during our study of the holy text" (www.sistersinislam.org.my).[4]

"It simply won't work", Toni insisted, referring to Esack's argument that in order to address contemporary issues it is necessary to go beyond the Islamic texts. "It is fine to do what Esack did as an academic exercise, but the reality in advocacy is that, when you try and work it on the ground, it just won't work", she said, and lamented the gap between academics and practically engaged activists.

As an NGO, SIS has a number of objectives. Among these are raising public awareness of women's rights in Islam, offering legal support to aggrieved individual women, and political advocacy for the reform of Islamic law in Malaysia. SIS recognizes the need for public support and awareness in order to effect change in the views that Malaysians, in particular Muslim Malaysians, have of the place of women in Islam. One type of activity that SIS organizes regularly is "training". I attended one of these training sessions for which the audience members were practising journalists. The purpose of the two-day workshop was to inform journalists of social and legal trends in Islam in Malaysia and, in particular, to illuminate the methods of Quranic interpretation and Syariah law-making.

THE INTERPRETATION OF THE QURAN

One of SIS's main strategies is demonstrating the human, rather than divine nature of textual interpretation. The male bias in interpretations of Islamic texts is one of the elements that SIS attempted to illuminate for the journalists in their workshop held in May 2005. One example used to illustrate this was the verse that is often cited to justify the idea that witnesses of *zinna* must be four males. This is the case in Pakistani law and the Hudud bills of PAS (see Chapter 3). These laws also enable a woman who accuses a man of raping her and who cannot produce four witnesses to be charged herself with false accusation of *zinna* (which has also been the case in Pakistan; see Khan 2003). If found guilty, she may be flogged.

Toni explained that it is important to know that Arabic is a gendered language. After examining the verse just mentioned in Arabic and paying attention to the pronouns, Toni demonstrated that only *men* who falsely charge women with *zinna* can be flogged (see Photo 2). The interpretation made by PAS and Pakistan is flatly wrong.

For the thirty or so journalists and authors present, this was a surprising disclosure. One participant asked, "But who gives them the power to interpret the verse like that?" "We all do", replied another participant, "because we never challenge it". Another SIS member, Nik Noriani, pointed out that the verse in its context had a sound purpose. She told the participants that, while the verse tells us that illicit sex is wrong, it is ultimately a personal matter and that this is evinced by the nigh impossibility of finding four witnesses to testify to having witnessed the act. Indeed, the greater sin is accusing someone of *zinna* because without the almost impossible four witnesses, such an accusation will draw a harsh punishment of its own. Far from articulating the punishment for *zinna*, the verse is in fact an affirmation of privacy.

THE INTERPRETATION OF THE *HADITH*

Along with the Quran, another source of Islamic jurisprudence are *Hadith*. Whereas the Quran is the word of God transmitted through the Prophet Muhammad, *Hadith* are the sayings and deeds of the Prophet, God's "perfect exemplar". The *Hadith* were systematically collected by various people, largely during the eighth century CE. Among the most well known of these collectors is Al-Bukhari who lived about two centuries after the Prophet. The collected *Hadith* were passed down orally and when they came to be recorded, the chain of transmission, its *isnad*, was likewise recorded.

Owing to the powerful legitimacy that a *Hadith* can lend to a person's viewpoint, politically and personally expedient *Hadith* proliferated. Within Islamic orthodoxy there are methods by which *Hadith* are determined as being credible or otherwise. For example, a *Hadith* is more credible if more people recalled it with the same links in its *isnad*. A *Hadith* was to be rejected if one of the chains of transmission was regarded as disreputable.

With this in mind, in her presentation at the workshop for journalists, Toni examined a famous *Hadith* that is frequently used to justify preventing women from holding leadership positions. The *Hadith*, as it was presented, was:

> Usamah bin Haisam related to us: Auf related to us from al Hassan (al-Bashri) from Abu Bakra. He said "Allah has made me see through

the kalimah from the Prophet … when I wanted to participate in the Camel War. That when the news reached the Prophet that the Persians had appointed Kisra's daughter as their leader, the Prophet said, 'Never shall a nation prosper under the leadership of a woman.'" Sahih al-Bukhari.

Toni first drew attention to the links in the chain of transmission and reminded the participants that "[i]f one of them is known to be unreliable or inconsistent in their reporting, then the whole *hadith tak pakai* [cannot be accepted]." "And", Toni continued, "Abu Bakra was once flogged for telling lies" (see also Mernissi 1991, pp. 60–61). Similarly, one should be wary of the *Hadith* from the popular transmitter Abu Hurayra.

Abu Hurayra means "Father of the little female cat". This was the nickname given to him by the Prophet because Abu Hurayra carried around a little cat which he adored (Mernissi 1991, p. 71). He is regarded by many as having a pronounced dislike of women and dogs and a number of misogynist and anti-canine *Hadith* originate from him.

At the SIS journalist training, Nik Noriani recounted that there is a *Hadith* attributed to Abu Hurayra in which he said that the Prophet Muhammed had said that horses, women, and certain kinds of houses bring bad luck. However, A'isha, probably the most celebrated of the Prophet's wives, frequently had to correct or deny Abu Hurayra's *Hadith*. With regard to this *Hadith*, Nik Noriani explained, Abu Hurayra had heard only half of it. According to A'isha, the Prophet had said that "God condemns those who say horses, women, and certain houses bring bad luck" (see also Mernissi 1991, p. 76).

ISLAMIC FUNDAMENTALS

On one occasion, I went with Toni to a bookstore in a large mall. In the bookstore there was a section of books on Islam. Among these was a children's colouring book on the cover of which was a simple mosque of a style that was, according to Toni, like those first built in Malaysia. However, upon opening the book, Toni was dismayed, though not surprised, at the mosques that were drawn inside for children to colour in. Unlike the mosque on the front cover, every mosque inside was of apparently Middle Eastern architecture and the little boy and girl who were recurring characters in the book were dressed in Middle Eastern garb. Toni noted that there was an increasing trend for mosques in Malaysia to be built in a style reminiscent of the Middle East rather than older local styles (an observation also noted by van Dijk 2010).

The conflation of Arabic culture with Islam that concerned Toni is a concern for many Muslims, especially those who may be regarded, for wont of better terms, liberal or progressive Muslims. For these Muslims, the distinction between what is Arabic and what is Islamic is an important one as it separates what is superficially Islamic with what they take to be its essence.

Contrary to popular negative representations of Islam, members of SIS argue that Islam accords rights to women that were far in advance of the West until relatively recently. In the context of the Prophet and his revelations, these rights were revolutionary. However, because the positions of authority in Islamic societies have since been held by men, the subsequent laws and interpretations have buried many of these advances in women's rights.

A frequently cited example of an ongoing asymmetry in gender relations in Islam is the relative ease with which Muslim men can divorce their wives, but the difficulty that women have in divorcing their husbands. An example that came to prominence in 2003 was the case in which a Syariah judge deemed as legitimate an affirmation of divorce made by a husband via a mobile phone text message.[5] This decision, according to members of SIS, was utterly unIslamic because it was against the fundamental Islamic principles of justice, equality, and, in particular, dignity. For SIS, any formal compliance with the received dictates of Islam is unIslamic if the predictable result of an act transgresses these fundamental principles.

In October 2004 I spoke with Abdul Mohaimin Ayus, then lecturer in law at the International Islamic University of Malaysia. While not sharing the views of SIS, he related to me a story that likewise illustrated the potential for restrictive interpretations of Islamic rules to lead to fundamental Islamic principles to be contravened. He told me of a newspaper article he had once read in which it was reported that a man had seen a dog stuck between two walls. The dog was unable to move and the man called the emergency services. However, this man was told that nobody could help the dog that day because the only people on duty were Muslims (many of whom regard dogs as polluting animals). "I got angry at that report", he told me. "People think there is a definitive ruling on all matters, but there is not. There are exceptions we have to consider."

He continued with a personal anecdote. He told me that after he had moved into a new house, the previous owners had left behind their dog. This dog kept approaching him and was evidently hungry. He asked his wife if there were some left-overs with which he could feed it. He also observed that the poor animal was always scratching and itching and that he could not bear to see the dog in such misery. He thus bought some dog shampoo, tied up the dog and bathed it. Afterwards, Mohaimin told me, the dog appeared happy and was jumping about.

Mohaimin then explained to me that there are a number of *Hadith* that relate to dogs. One was to the effect that a dog at one's house will restrain angels from entering it. Another was that one could keep a hunting dog. Another again was that if a person were to throw a stone at a neighbour's dog and if the neighbour were to take offence, then the person who threw the stone will not enter paradise. Yet another was that by a well there was a dog which was obviously thirsty. Seeing the dog, a man scooped water from the well with his shoe and let the dog drink from it. The Prophet said of that man that he would enter paradise. Finally, it is also said, Mohaimin told me, that if one touches a wet dog, then one must conduct a special ablution using seven pots, one of which contains mud and the other six water. Mohaimin told me that after washing the dog, he performed this ablution. He explained, "I took the *Hadith* in total — not just one." The task, he said more generally, was understanding Islam as a whole.[6]

In a similar vein, one SIS member, referring to "fundamentalists" who insist on formal compliance with "Islamic" rules without regard to more basic tenets of Islam, asked, "Who are the real *fundamentalists*? They are not the real fundamentalists." That is, those normally called fundamentalists are in fact the ones who ignore Islam's fundamental foundations of justice, equality, and dignity. For many, one occasion when these fundamentals were ignored — indeed, it is regarded by many as a landmark moment in egregious and unwarranted moral policing — was the raid on a nightclub by the Jabatan Agama Islam Wilayah Persekutuan (Federal Territory Islamic Department; hereafter JAWI).

THE JAWI RAID

On 20 January 2005, JAWI conducted a raid on Zouk nightclub to nab Muslims behaving in ways regarded as unIslamic and breaking laws that pertain only to Muslims (such as having consumed alcohol). As a result of this raid, over one hundred young Muslims were arrested for indecent behaviour and alcohol consumption. When details of the raid came to light, a furore ensued over the legitimacy of such a raid and the conduct of the officers involved. As a consequence, 50 NGOs and 220 individuals formed a coalition called Malaysians Against Moral Policing. This coalition called for a commission to review Malaysia's civil and Islamic laws, in particular those that infringed fundamental liberties.

The detainees in this raid had to wait as long as ten hours to be processed. The males were processed more quickly and were made to take a breathalyser test. The females, however, were subjected to what some of the detainees described as humiliating treatment. Reports that appeared both in the mainstream Malaysian press as well as non-government-controlled news websites revealed a number of details of sexual harassment and rough handling.

The JAWI officers commanded the female detainees to parade in front of them so that the officers could assess whether they were decently dressed. Numerous news reports described the male officers as ogling and photographing women who wore "sexy" clothing. One detainee reported to a local paper that an officer had commented "*ini musim panas agaknya sebab dia orang pakai baju puting-puting semua nampak*" (it must be the hot season because they are wearing skimpy clothes such that even their nipples can be seen). Elsewhere, it was reported that the officers made degrading statements and asked inappropriate questions about some of the females' genitals (Kent 2005). The then Secretary of Malaysia's National Human Rights Society (known as HAKAM), Elizabeth Wong, reported that in addition to a "cat-walk procedure" and an unusually long processing time, the female detainees were also subjected to leering and "the persistence of JAWI officers in asking for the telephone numbers of the women in custody" outside of regular protocol (Wong E. 2005).

To those freed without charge, the JAWI officers issued "'summonses' for counselling sessions ... under the guise of conducting an investigation under Section 58(1) of the Syariah Criminal Procedure (Federal Territories) Act 1997" (ibid.). The officers also threatened the detainees with arrest if they did not appear at these sessions. However, in a written statement in response to a possible challenge over the legality of the summonses and the threatened arrest, JAWI "clarified" that the sessions were voluntary (ibid.).

There were numerous reactions to these raids in the mainstream press and the Internet media. One comment made a number of times was that the behaviour of the JAWI officers had brought Islam into disrepute and may have turned young people against Islam. Zainah Anwar, the then Executive Director of SIS, argued that the laws used to arrest the young people have "no basis in Islamic legal theory and practice and violate fundamental guarantees in the Federal Constitution" (Arfa'eza and Nurul 2005). Indeed, the raid and the laws that allowed it were counter to the fundamental Islamic principles of justice, equality, and dignity (ibid.).

Others supported such raids, but suggested that the officers could have conducted themselves better. The Kuala Lumpur wing of PAS Youth, for instance, supported the raid which they described as being conducted with "sincerity and utmost dedication" (Malaysiakini.com 2005*d*). Angkatan Belia Islam Malaysia (the Malaysian Islamic Youth Movement), which was once led by Anwar Ibrahim, called for the establishment of a religious unit in the Malaysian police force because "a combination of professionalism, educational foundation and strong sense of morality could boost the quality of service and, in turn, change negative public perceptions of the police force" (Malaysiakini.com 2005*e*).

Following these raids, a joint-statement titled, "The State Has No Role in Policing Morality", was prepared by the Malaysians Against Moral Policing coalition. In it they expressed concern over the increased "role of the state in policing the morality of its citizens". Particularly disturbing for them was the above described raid as well as, among other things, the arrest that occurred around the time of a transgender individual on private property, and talk of State-sanctioned volunteer "snoop squads" that would spy on people and report moral infractions (see also Darshini 2006).

In their joint statement, the NGOs expressed concern that laws pertaining to morality were vague and open to "interpretation and abuse by enforcement officers, which can lead to selective prosecution and victimization, usually of those from a marginalised class, gender and/or community" (SIS Forum Asia 2005). Instead, signatories to the statement "affirm that morality is a matter best dealt with by individuals and their families".[7] The joint statement also affirmed the signatories' protest against the use of "state instruments, and the individuals and groups enlisted as their surrogates, to regulate morality. How people dress and where, how and with whom they socialise are personal choices" (ibid.).

At a related forum, lawyer Haris bin Mohamed Ibrahim, expressed his grave concern over Article 12 of the Federal Territories Syariah Criminal Offences Bill 1996. This Article states,

> Any person who gives, propagates or disseminates any opinion concerning Islamic teachings, Islamic Law or any issue, contrary to any fatwa for the time being in force in the Federal Territories shall be guilty of offence and shall on conviction be liable to a fine not exceeding three thousand ringgit or to imprisonment for a term not exceeding two years or to both.

Haris, commenting on this law and the makers of it, said, "Now you analyse this, it means Muslims cannot think. That's frightening. Who authorized them? The answer is that we sat back as these laws were promulgated. We sat back as bit by bit our freedoms were taken away from us."

He went on to say that, "[i]t is incumbent now upon every Muslim, whether you're from Umno Puteri [UMNO's women's wing] or Umno Youth or the head of the party to sit up, to take stock and admit our mistakes in having not stopped the slippery slide down. We must reclaim our stake in this country" (Fauwaz 2005).

The notion of reclaiming Malaysia from laws that are ostensibly founded in Islam gives rise to a dilemma in advocacy, however. Firstly, much of the non-Muslim population will feel that they have no stake in the affairs of Muslims. Islamist Muslim groups and individuals frequently assert that commentary on or criticism of Islamic affairs by non-Muslims is inappropriate. At a forum on the topic of moral policing in May 2005, a PAS member of parliament was reported to have closed her presentation by saying to non-Muslims in the audience, "unto you your religion and unto us our religion".[8] This comment was reported as being an undisguised message to the effect that "non-Muslims should hug the sidelines and not comment on syariah laws" (Pereira 2005).

Furthermore, repeated government affirmations that religion and race are "sensitive issues" and a matter of national security, also echo here. As one letter to the editor of Malaysiakini.com wrote, "If the Muslims feel that they are being unfairly persecuted, then it is only they that can fix the problem. We non-Muslims are not allowed to question their religious beliefs or actions. The infamous ISA is there to ensure that" (Davidson 2005). Social activists in Malaysia regard the fracturing of Malaysian society into ethnic and religious sub-categories as the result of the successful "divide and rule" tactics of the Malaysian government — a tactic it inherited from Malaysia's colonial administration.

Concomitantly, there is raft of discourse and interdictions from within Islamic orthodoxy that can be deployed to dissuade criticism by Muslims of political, legal, and social developments in Islam. Zainah has written of a "shroud of silence" that veils the making of Syariah law in Malaysia, as well as fear among Muslims of speaking out for fear of, among other things, being accused of being "anti-Islam, and accused of questioning the word of God" (2005, p. 126; see also Martinez 2004, p. 47). Previously we have seen that the charge of *kafir* (unbeliever) was used against those who did not accept PAS's Hudud Bill (see Chapter 3). Likewise has the charge of blasphemy been used. And, as mentioned above, contradicting a fatwa is an offence.

Thus it is evident that working within the Islamic framework is fraught with difficulties. Working within it can invite the criticism, sometimes levelled at SIS, that by engaging with it one legitimizes its place in public discourse and politics. Instead, to such critics, the legitimacy of the Islamic discourse in the public sphere needs to be challenged.

The entry of Islam into the public sphere has many causes, including the nature of Malaysia's electoral system. In the next chapter I will describe how Malaysia's electoral system has facilitated Islamization. I will show how it has, perhaps falsely, indicated popular support for Islamic politics and thus legitimized Islam's prominent place in the public sphere. How this occurs, and how civil society has reacted to the unwelcomed effects of Malaysia's electoral system, will be described in the following chapter.

Engaging with the electoral system is also not without its difficulties and dilemmas, as we shall see. In part owing to these problems, and likewise because of the difficulties associated with other realms such as the courts, SIS perceives a continuing necessity in operating within an Islamic framework to attain their goal of enhancing Muslim women's rights. Working within this framework, as SIS members are aware, is fraught and they are at risk of being politically attacked by orthodox Muslims on various grounds. To lessen the likelihood of such rejection SIS uses orthodox interpretative tools and texts to reach their conclusions about Islam's position on given matters — conclusions which may themselves be unorthodox, but are at least hermeneutically sound. Meanwhile, the suggestion of Farid Esack to go beyond the texts in finding solutions to contemporary problems is untenable from an advocacy perspective, not to mention unacceptable to many Islamically oriented activists themselves.

Notes

1. This *Hadith* can be found in *Sahih Bukhari*, Volume 8, Book 82, Number 806.
2. In April 2004 *CBS News* televised and *The New Yorker* published pictures of American soldiers abusing and sexually humiliating Muslim Iraqi prisoners in Abu Ghraib prison in Iraq. These images were then republished and televised around the world and the behaviour of the American military personnel in the images drew widespread condemnation.
3. Verse 16:69 states, "There issues from within [the bees'] bodies a drink of varying colours, wherein is healing for men". Translation of Yusuf Ali.
4. Accessed 19 February 2010.
5. In order to effect a divorce in Syariah law in Malaysia, a husband must pronounce "I divorce you" to his wife three times. The said text-message was taken by the court to constitute one of those occasions.
6. There are many Muslims who regard Islam as having no prohibition against dogs whatsoever and argue that, far from regarding dogs negatively, the Quran

portrays the dogs favourably (see, for example, Syed A. A. 2008, pp. 191–200).

7. The signatories to the joint statement called for:

    (a) The repeal of provisions in religious and municipal laws that deny citizens their fundamental right to privacy, freedom of speech and expression, and those that overlap with the federal Penal Code;

    (b) The appointment of a committee to monitor the process of repealing these laws, including representation from women's groups, human rights groups, civil society organizations, progressive religious scholars, and constitutional experts;

    (c) The strengthening of our pluralism through community dialogue around morals in our society, rather than the divisiveness bred by sub-contracting of moral policing and neighbours spying on neighbours.

8. This remark would appear to be an allusion to verse 109:6 of the Quran which states, "Unto you your religion, and unto me my religion." Translation of Marmaduke Pickthall.

8

ELECTORAL ENGAGEMENTS

This chapter seeks to demonstrate how the electoral system in Malaysia has facilitated the Islamization I have thus far described, how it is biased towards maintaining BN rule, and how some elements of civil society have tried to advocate for electoral reform.

My description of the Malaysian electoral system will begin with a discussion of the socio-political impacts of the "first-past-the-post" electoral system which is in effect in Malaysia. I am concerned to show how it constrains the diversification of voices and how it encouraged PAS's declaration in 2004 that it would strive to establish an Islamic state. I will then examine how the practice of Malaysian elections further serves to constrain minority voices and to confirm the ongoing rule of the BN and the socio-political status quo. This discussion shall be undertaken with reference to the campaign of one PKR candidate during the 2004 elections. I will then examine how Malaysians have reacted to these electoral constraints and their effects by describing the heightened social activism that surrounded the 2008 elections. The cause of this social activism lay in dissatisfaction with government policy and unaccountability and, importantly, in the effects of Islamization. The reduction in democratic space resulted in citizens seeking ways to participate in democracy beyond participating directly in elections. I discuss the large public rallies that took place before the elections and the Women's Candidacy Initiative.

THE FIRST-PAST-THE-POST SYSTEM

In Malaysian elections, the winners of seats in the lower house are decided according to a simple first-past-the-post system. For the lower house, whichever candidate garners the most votes in an electorate wins the seat and any vote for a losing candidate has no representational value. The members of the upper house are largely appointed by the Sultan, and the house is not composed of members of parties in proportion to the popular vote.

For the purposes of my discussion here, I will compare the first-past-the-post system with what is often referred to as proportional representation. In short, this differs from first-past-the-post systems in that, a vote for a losing candidate or party is not wasted and retains representational value. Thus, for example, if a party were to lose every seat it contested, if it managed to nevertheless win 10 per cent of the total vote, that party would gain 10 per cent of the seats in the upper house of Parliament.

In the first-past-the-post system, because any vote for a candidate who does not win has no value whatsoever (sometimes called a wasted vote), it makes no difference to the outcome of the elections whether a candidate has won or lost by the slimmest of margins or by the largest. Hypothetically, even if Party A were to lose every contest only by the slimmest of margins, Party A would be completely unrepresented. There are significant consequences for this which will shortly become apparent.

In a hypothetical country which has a population that is politically divided between conservatives and liberals, if a given seat was contested by one conservative and two liberal parties, the conservative party would be at an advantage because the liberal vote in that seat would be split. It would always be preferable for a party of a given kind to be the only such party contesting a seat. Ideally, if one were a liberal party candidate, one would wish to be the sole candidate from a liberal party with a number of conservative candidates. The liberal candidate would scoop the liberal vote while the conservative vote would be divided.

In such circumstances, what one might expect to see is that, among themselves, liberal and conservative parties would decide before the campaign period who would contest which seat and to not contest where another politically similar party was contesting. As a consequence, any given contest would be likely to feature only two candidates — a liberal and conservative candidate from one or another liberal or conservative party. (In a proportional representation electoral system, the need to avoid splitting the vote is greatly reduced as losing votes still have representational value in the upper house.)

Similar but more complex pre-election bargaining takes place in Malaysia. Rather than liberals versus conservatives, in Malaysia the first axis of division is over whether a candidate belongs to a BN or to a non-BN party. The second axis is ethnicity.

In any given contest in Malaysia, BN coalition parties never contest the same seat and opposition parties usually agree not to compete against each other for a given seat so as not to divide the anti-BN vote. If, for instance, a PAS candidate and a PKR candidate were both to stand against a BN candidate in a given seat, the protest vote against the BN would be divided and the opposition parties would have mutually undermined their chances of winning. As a result, most contests for seats are "two corner fights" because in "three corner fights" opposition candidates tend to knock each other out. For this reason, a voter in Alor Setar in the state of Kedah, for example, would have had to choose in 2004 between voting for either a PAS candidate or a BN candidate for federal Parliament. There was no PKR or DAP option.

In Malaysia, however, political parties usually represent or are seen to represent particular ethnic groups. In peninsular Malaysia, with the exception of the BN's Malaysian Indian Congress, the other main parties are associated with either Chinese or Malays. The MCA, Gerakan, and the DAP are Chinese oriented or dominated, although in the latter two cases, the discourses are multi-ethnic. UMNO and PAS are Malay oriented. PKR, the newest party of significance, is an exception to the rule. While the party heads have been Malay (Anwar Ibrahim and, before him, his wife, Wan Azizah Wan Ismail), it has successfully cultivated leaders from the three largest ethnic groups and ostensibly eschews ethnic and religious chauvinism.

One consequence of such a system is that smaller ethnic groups, special interest parties, and parties whose frame is entirely unrelated to ethnicity have been unable to develop. For one, "mosquito" parties, as small unestablished (and electorally inconsequential) parties are sometimes referred to in Malaysia, would also be unlikely to garner much support. This is because a voter is unlikely to expend a precious vote on an unlikely party — however much more he or she might prefer its politics — but would rather spend it supporting a candidate from an established party that had better chances of winning. Furthermore, from a candidate's perspective, competing as a weak candidate would also play into the hands of the ruling coalition by splitting any anti-BN vote and so could potentially do further damage to one's cause. And additionally, there is no point competing in Malaysia with an eye to forming a presence in the upper house. The effect of the first-past-the-post system in reducing party diversity is well known among political scientists. Proportional representation, meanwhile, "makes it easier for minor parties to be represented" and a "greater diversity of interests and perspectives to be aired" (Blais 1991, p. 244).

Another consequence of the first-past-the-post system is that, with the variety of parties being so constrained, individuals wishing to bring about political change may be channelled into supporting one of the few available opposition parties. One individual I interviewed noted to me that a relative of his was the head of PAS in his village, but that the only reason he was with PAS was "because he hates UMNO. He's not pious at all! He just hates UMNO."

Therefore, because electoral choice is greatly constrained in Malaysia, it is difficult to interpret election results. Is a vote for PAS an indication of support for their agenda? Or is it merely a protest vote against the BN? Furthermore, nuanced readings of popular sentiment are further hampered by the relative lack of public opinion surveying.

In the midst of the Reformasi movement and significant discontent with the BN, PAS in 1999 won twenty-seven of the sixty-three seats it contested and took control of the state of Terengganu and retained Kelantan. In the period between the 1999 and 2004 elections, PAS leaders commonly spoke of their plan to establish an Islamic state and released their "blueprint" for such a state (see Chapter 3). In 2004 PAS used its 1999 success as leverage to broker for the right to contest more seats. However, of the eighty-four seats it contested in 2004, and in the context of Abdullah Badawi's political "honeymoon period", it won only seven. Leading into the 2008 elections, PAS toned down greatly its Islamic state discourse, affirmed the place of non-Muslims in Malaysia, and behaved more conciliatorily towards the DAP and PKR.

What appears apparent in the shifting approach of PAS between 1999 and 2008 is that it (mis)read electoral success as implying support for its agenda. Taking its 1999 success as an affirmation, PAS became more outspoken about its desire to establish an Islamic state. But taking 2004 as a rejection, PAS toned its Islamic state discourse down.

In the period between 1999 and 2004, the apparent ascendance of the Islamist movement saw a number of attempted counter-manoeuvres by UMNO. One such manoeuvre was Dr Mahathir's Islamic state declaration in 2001. Another was Dr Mahathir's choice of successor, Abdullah Badawi, who has a degree in Islamic studies and comes from a family of religious figures. Regardless of the actual level of support for Islamist politics (which, I have shown, is not deducible from election results), these moves certainly elevated the legitimacy of Islam in the political sphere and made the Islamic discourse one that could not be ignored.

Whereas the above addresses the effects of the first-past-the-post system per se, that discussion does not capture how the practice of democracy is further constrained by the nature of the political environment in Malaysia. This environment, which is hostile to wider participation by the public, serves either to channel those who wish to protest against government practices and authoritarianism into established parties and entrenched party structures, or to lead activists to try to work outside the electoral framework and to transform it in various ways. After describing these practical impediments, I will go on to describe how in 1999 and 2008, the Women's Candidacy Initiative sought to transform the electoral framework, and how a number of large rallies prior to the 2008 elections were exercises in non-electoral democracy and, in the case of one rally, called for reforms to the conduct of elections.

PRACTICAL IMPEDIMENTS TO POLITICAL PARTICIPATION

During the campaign period of the March 2004 election, I followed the campaign of PKR candidate, Sivarasa Rasiah. Before joining PKR and becoming its vice-president, Sivarasa was also a high-profile lawyer and activist. In 2004 he contested the seat of Petaling Jaya South which was held by Donald Lim, a BN coalition candidate from the constituent MCA.

On 17 March 2004, four days prior to polling day, Sivarasa Rasiah was to have a *ceramah*. A *ceramah* in the context of an election is essentially a meet-your-candidate session. It is held at a public place and five or so speakers, including the candidate, will introduce the candidate and speak about pertinent issues. *Ceramah* are an important means by which opposition party candidates make contact with the electorate because the mainstream media is under the control of the BN coalition (see also Transparency International 2008, pp. 203–204). Coverage in the print and electronic media (excepting the internet) is poor for opposition parties and when it does occur, the reporting is often unfavourable. Indeed, control of the media is one of the often cited three Ms that the BN has at its disposal, the other two being money and government machinery (i.e. State infrastructure).

Although opposition parties still make appeals to the mainstream media by supplying them with press statements and by having press conferences, opposition party candidates must employ other strategies for disseminating their message. These other means include displaying posters in public places, leafleting mailboxes, "loudhailing" (addressing the public using a mega-phone), personally meeting constituents, and holding *ceramah*. *Ceramah* are often held outdoors, in the evening, and require a police permit. This permit is valid only for a particular time and place.

Sivarasa's campaign team organized a *ceramah* for almost every night of the eight-day campaign period. For 17 March a desirable venue had been secured with police permission some days earlier. In addition to claiming a strategic position, various logistical considerations must be taken into account when preparing a *ceramah*, including the provision of a viable stage and appropriate lighting and sound amplification.

On this day I had followed Sivarasa and a few others as they went on a meet-and-greet tour of Taman Medan, one of the poorer areas within Petaling Jaya South. When we returned to the *bilik gerakan* (campaign centre) we were informed by a harried campaigner that the police had revoked the permit for the original venue and relocated the PKR *ceramah* to a *padang* (field, often used for recreation). The good venue that PKR had booked was going to be used by Donald Lim and his team.

Some volunteers went to the new *ceramah* site while other volunteers remained at the *bilik gerakan* to continue other tasks such as making banners out of posters, placing these banners around the constituency, constructing wooden signposts that could be hammered into the ground, monitoring the media, and organizing the days to come.

When we arrived at the venue I could see that, far from the prime location which was the original venue, the *padang* was in utter darkness and looked desolate. Its redeeming feature was that it was bordered by houses from which residents might emerge out of curiosity. Those setting up the venue began turning a battered old lorry, which had been hired for the occasion, into a stage and stringing up as many banners and posters as possible to make it festive and evidently a PKR *ceramah*. After some fretfulness during the setting-up of the electrical generator and the lighting and sound, the stage began to take shape and became functional.

Despite the late notice that the residents in the area had of the *ceramah* — some were alerted by a volunteer driving around and loudhailing into houses — I was surprised to see approximately twenty to thirty people in attendance. However, as an effective means of "reaching the people", and as an effective use of manpower and resources, I had my doubts. Apart from the forced venue change, there are two other aspects of this *ceramah* that are noteworthy.

First, present at this *ceramah*, loitering behind the rest of the audience, was a member of the Special Branch of the police. He was pointed out to me by some of the other volunteers and was distinctive by his conspicuous attempt to appear inconspicuous. This man who frequently spoke into his mobile phone and never made eye-contact with anyone, was the source of little more than mere recognition by the other volunteers who troubled themselves only in pointing him out to me. Indeed, surveillance by Special Branch officers, who are commonly referred to as SBs, is the norm for any public event organized by an opposition party or an NGO.

A second noteworthy occurrence at the *ceramah* was that, while one of the PKR volunteers was taking photographs for the campaign website, he took a photo of a woman who subsequently became distressed. I was told that she was distressed because she did not want to be photographed at an opposition party event.

When the *ceramah* concluded I returned to the *bilik gerakan* and joined a few dedicated volunteers who were seated on the floor, folding leaflets to be distributed the following day. While doing this, a film crew, purportedly from Bernama, the government-owned news agency, came ostensibly to do a story.

At one point during the film crew's visit, I observed the cameraman filming at close proximity the lists and charts that were posted on the walls and doors. These contained details relating to campaign volunteers, tasks, and dates. I asked one of the experienced volunteers why they would be filming the wall so closely. Ann James, Sivarasa's wife, who was sitting next to me, remarked merrily that I had been "corrupted". I asked her what she meant and she explained that now I, too, was suspicious of people but that, indeed, "they could be undercover SBs for all we know."

Clear from the above account are a couple of things. One is that the difficulties associated with participating in an opposition party campaign, including for many even being seen in the proximity of such a campaign, means that many citizens would feel disinclined to lend practical support for a non-BN candidate, thus hampering the functioning of the electoral process. Another is that, in addition to effects of the first-past-the-post system described earlier, the difficulties facing opposition parties further distort the ability for the electoral system to represent the political will of voters. There are many rules and laws that impede opposition parties far more than ruling coalition parties. Furthermore, laws are often enforced when opposition parties appear to infringe them while they are overlooked when the BN transgress them. Such is the situation that William Case writes that "rule-bending has become so pervasive that the regime must be adjudged as falling outside the 'democratic' category altogether and belonging to a separate category of pseudodemocracy" (2001, p. 46). Indeed, "a set of institutions has emerged that, while formally democratic, in fact yield a pattern of executive supremacy, UMNO party dominance, and ethnic preference for Malays" (ibid.). Some of these institutions, such as the police and the Electoral Commission, are demonstrably not independent of the ruling coalition despite being ostensible functionaries of the State and not partisan.

The election results of 2008, in which the BN lost its two-thirds majority in federal Parliament and lost control of several states, may appear at first glance to indicate that the biases in favour of the BN are not as strong as I and others have portrayed them. However, I would argue that these biases, while somewhat tempered by the effects of the electoral reform protests in 2007, which I will describe later, continue to be strong. The results of the 2008 election in fact indicate that the feeling of discontent among voters was almost stronger than the biases could contain. Without past and ongoing impediments to opposition party participation such as those I describe below, the strength of the BN would have been weakened quite some time ago and possibly would have lost power in 2008 if not earlier.

The Media

One of these impediments is the biased coverage of political news in the mainstream media. This is the first of the BN's "three Ms". The mainstream print and electronic media require their operating licences to be renewed annually by the government. Thus, those media that are not owned directly by government interests are otherwise cowed by coercive legislation in the form of the Printing Presses and Publications Act. As of its latest revision in 1988, judicial review of a minister's decision to revoke or deny a permit is impossible if the minister is satisfied that public order may be compromised by the publication (Anuar 2002, p. 128). The threat of suspension is real as, in 1987, three local newspapers, *The Star, Sin Chew Jit Poh*, and *Watan*, had their licences suspended. In 2002 some issues of the international newsmagazines *Newsweek, Time*, and the *Far Eastern Economic Review* were blocked from distribution in Malaysia. Within the two months prior to the elections in 2008, control of *The Sun* newspaper was taken over by Vincent Tan, an entrepreneur well known for his close links to government. *The Sun*, described in one report as "a feisty free tabloid that has become popular in recent years because of its often bold coverage of government corruption, politics and religious issues" (Lopez 2008), had, prior to being taken over, been publicly criticized by government ministers for being pro-opposition.

Immediately after the take-over, editorial policy changed and its criticisms of the government were muted.

The ISA has also been deployed against media staff on the grounds that they compromised national security (see Anuar 2002, p. 151, and passim. for a fuller discussion of the state of the media in Malaysia; see also Transparency International 2008, pp. 203–204). Otherwise editors have been dismissed for displeasing the wrong minister (Case 2005, p. 218).

Even though Malaysians are often sceptical of news reports and aware that the media is biased in its reporting, it can nevertheless influence the political climate in anticipation of events such as the 2004 elections by creating an atmosphere of unease and trepidation. The media frequently carried stories in separate articles in which BN politicians made references to Malaysia's inter-ethnic harmony. A number of critics of the government have suggested to me that the intention is to remind people of the riots of May 1969 which occurred days after the BN lost its two-thirds majority in Parliament, and to fuel the belief that ongoing BN rule was necessary for social stability. Syed Husin Ali, a former academic and current vice-president of PKR, has noted that "[i]n every election the government resorts to fear tactics by manipulating public memory of this tragedy" (Syed H. A. 2001, p. 126). During the 1999 Malaysian general elections, the media linked the political upheaval in Indonesia with the killings of Chinese there to suggest, according to some, that any support for the opposition in Malaysia may likewise lead to social instability, thus inclining voters towards retaining the incumbent government.

Money

The second of the BN's three Ms is its access to money. Although section 19 of the Elections Act constrains candidates from spending more than RM200,000 (US$59,000)[1] in their campaigns, it is widely assumed that in actuality, the amount spent by BN candidates far exceeds that limit (for similar comments with regard to the 1999 general elections, see Weiss 2000, p. 432; regarding the 2008 election, see for example Syed J.Z. 2008).

It is worth here relating a phenomenon I witnessed during the 2004 elections. One day during the campaign period I brought to the attention of Sivarasa's team that many BN billboards were having sections covered over (see Photo 3). The sections that were being covered were first those that said, *"Pilihan Yang Bijak: Barisan Nasional"* ("The Smart Choice: National Front"), and second, the section which showed the BN symbol next to a checked box, such as one would find on a voting form. One proffered explanation was that if the billboards were to be counted in the cost of the campaign budget, the limit would be evidently exceeded, and just on billboards alone. By covering the sections which indicated that the billboards were directly related to the elections, the BN could claim that they were general advertisements that were not related to any campaign.

Another important monetary aspect is that candidates must submit a deposit to the Electoral Commission. Malaysia's deposit is among the most expensive in the world (Brown 2005, p. 433), all the more so when the earning power of the ringgit is considered. For a federal parliament candidate, the total deposit is RM15,000 (US$4,400). By comparison, election deposits in Australia are AU$250 (US$225), in Canada C$200 (US$190), and in Ireland they are unconstitutional. (I might note that in Singapore, Malaysia's neighbour, election deposits are S$13,500 (US$9,560)). The size of the deposit in Malaysia makes it difficult for candidates from poorer opposition parties, as well as independents, to stand. The Women's Candidacy Initiative, as I shall describe below, saw these election deposits as particularly discriminatory against women who often earn less then men or are encouraged in Malaysia to remain housewives with little earning capacity.

Machinery

The third M refers to machinery. That is, BN's access to and manipulation of State bodies. Case notes that the government "makes uninhibited use of state facilities and government workers, especially in the Information Ministry and the Kemas (Community Development) Unit" (2001, p. 48). During the election, other bodies such as the Electoral Commission, which oversees the running of the election, appear to cooperate with the BN. I describe below one example of collusion between the BN and the Electoral Commission that occurred just two days before polling day in 2004.

Electoral Commission

Since carrying out its first redrawing of electoral boundaries in 1960 which dissatisfied the government, the Electoral Commission has lost much of its independence. Graham K. Brown writes that it is "now widely seen by critics as little more than a fig leaf for the government's desired manipulation of constituency boundaries" (2005, p. 433). Brown notes that these re-delineations have, since 1986, increased the political bias of the electoral system in favour of the BN (ibid., p. 430).

Active collusion of the Electoral Commission with the BN was evident in 2004. Prior to the commencement of the campaign period, the Electoral Commission had made clear that *pondok panas* were not permitted. A *pondok panas*, in the context of an election, is rather like a large tent set up nearby to polling stations (see Photo 4). At the *pondok panas*, voters can find out where it is they must go to vote and receive other related information.

In the days prior to the election, however, some volunteers as well as myself saw structures being erected near polling stations that looked as if they would be used as *pondok panas* on polling day. Our suspicion that collusion had occurred between the BN and the Electoral Commission was revealed to be justified when, two days prior to polling day the Electoral Commission announced that *pondok panas* were to be permitted. The erected structures were, indeed, used by the BN as their *pondok panas*. Given the late notice, Sivarasa's team was not able to set up their own *pondok panas*, although some opposition campaigns managed to establish some in time.

Prior to the 2008 election, the BN rushed through an amendment to the Constitution to enable the Election Commission Chairman to serve up until the age of sixty-six. This allowed the long-serving Tan Sri Abdul Rashid Abdul Rahman to oversee the Election Commission's activities in the 2008 elections. According to critics, such as the leader of the DAP, Lim Kit Siang, this more easily enabled the Electoral Commission's conducting of a biased election (Lim 2008). Also in the days prior to the elections, the Electoral Commission Chairman announced that the use of indelible ink on the fingers of those who have voted — which had been introduced for 2008 to prevent people from voting numerous times and which was introduced owing to civil society pressure (see below) — would be scrapped owing to concerns that criminals had smuggled in indelible ink and wished to derail the elections by inking people's fingers in advance of their voting. This move was widely regarded by civil society and opposition parties as a ruse to scrap the use of indelible ink to enable election cheating by multiple voting by individuals.

Police and the Special Branch

It is widely accepted that the police and the BN cooperate in ways detrimental to opposition parties. An example of this was given at the beginning of this chapter when the police revoked and reissued a permit for a *ceramah* to the disadvantage of Sivarasa's campaign and to the advantage of Donald Lim. But possibly the biggest disincentives to democratic participation come from the activities of Special Branch personnel, as well as other people who act as informants.

In his eminent ethnography, *Weapons of the Weak*, James C. Scott also notes the effect of SBs on political dissent in a rural Malay village. He describes how

> police from the Special Branch came twice to speak with Bashir and with the headman, Haji Jaafar. The visits had their intended effect, as I suspect they did in countless other villages on the rice plain. Many PAS members knew that a word from Bashir or the [village committee] could spell arrest and feared they would be victimized. As Mustapha noted, "Of course we're afraid; they want to crush (*menindas*) PAS" (Scott 1985, pp. 276–77).

SBs and police informants are a fact of life for political parties. In an interview, PKR candidate Xavier Jayakumar revealed to me that there were a number of people helping in his campaign in 2004 who were almost certainly informants. They had come "out of the blue" to volunteer and seemed to loiter unnecessarily during meetings. When I asked why he did not get rid of them, he replied that he was so short of helpers that he could not afford to forgo their labour.

It was taken for granted by all the volunteers in Sivarasa's campaign that whatever they did or said could be monitored. When I enquired further about this, members of Sivarasa's campaign team responded with a relatively uniform nonchalance. "So far as we care", said Latheefa Koya, Sivarasa's campaign manager, "they can listen because we're not doing anything illegal. We don't mind."

On another occasion, Sivarasa explained to me that one thing he does when SBs are at an event is to openly acknowledge their presence. He went on to tell me that, if there are people who are unfamiliar with Malaysia or with SBs, he will even personally and politely introduce them to the officers. He does this firstly to make the unacquainted aware of the SBs' presence and also to demystify their potentially menacing aura.

However blasé those who are used to it may be, State surveillance poses a significant deterrent to regular citizens' participation in and support for opposition political parties. For the woman described at the beginning of this chapter, being photographed just watching a public *ceramah* was enough to distress her. The deterrent would be greater still to actively volunteering for an opposition party candidate's campaign or even standing as a candidate.

The ubiquity of the belief that people around you may be SBs or police informants was made plain to me in a play by Huzir Sulaiman called

"*Election Day*" (published in Huzir 2002). The play, which I saw in 2004, is set during the 1999 elections and involves four main characters who are spoken about in a monologue: one former rising star in PAS, one DAP volunteer, the apparently politically unaffiliated monologist (all three of these characters are house-mates), and a love interest. Of pertinence here is that the former two characters suffer repeated setbacks in their lives which turn out to be the result of the deliberate undermining by the monologist who reveals himself at the end as a police informant.

That an audience could assimilate such a storyline suggests the pervasiveness of the anxiety that even intimate acquaintances could be police informants. Spying and surveillance form a part of the Malaysian national consciousness, especially when it comes to political involvement. I might note that one volunteer had revealed to me that, over the years, she had uncovered a few informants, but in the tense atmosphere of the 1999 elections, had also wrongly accused a good friend.

Retribution and Surveillance

Retribution for anti-establishment views, and especially the fear of same, is a common concern in Malaysia. In 2005 one academic claimed he lost his job because of his critical views of the government. Another academic, who had likewise been critical, only won the continuation of his tenure after public outcry when this continuation was initially denied (Welsh 2005). In 1999 the tenure of Chandra Muzaffar, former Director of the Centre for Civilisational Dialogue, Universiti Malaya, was not renewed after his prominent role in the Reformasi movement. In 2008, the contract of the then principal for New Era College, Kua Kia Soong, who is also a human rights activist, was not renewed in not dissimilar circumstances.

The fear of personal retribution for voting against an oppressive government or party is certainly why the Universal Declaration of Human Rights states that ballots in elections must be secret. Up until 2008 Malaysian elections have not been secret. The serial numbers of the voters' ballot slips were recorded with the voters' names on the electoral roll so that, in theory, a vote could be traced back to the voter. Prior to polling day in 2008, a widely circulated SMS stated, "Your voting ballot has NO serial no. The govt CANNOT trace who you vote 4". While the practice of recording serial numbers on ballot slips was officially stopped in 2006, there were reports in 2008 of officers recording these numbers in some polling stations (Phang, L-A. 2008, p. 10). However, prior to 2006, and as is implied by the SMS message above, the presence of these serial numbers was seen as inhibiting people from voting for an opposition party candidate owing to the fear of their support being discovered (see also Case 2005, p. 222).

Sorting paranoia from objectively legitimate fears is difficult when concrete evidence of direct surveillance is difficult to obtain. What is important in the context of this chapter is that Malaysians — and not only activists and public figures — frequently experience government surveillance as ubiquitous and malevolent. Like others to whom I had spoken, members of Sivarasa's campaign team coped with surveillance in the same way they coped with SBs – by working within all relevant laws as far as possible.

Keeping within the law is not always possible, however. Many laws are vaguely worded and thus allow arbitrary interpretation and enforcement. Occasionally the rules are openly flouted as a deliberate act of defiance. One example during the 2004 election campaign was in connection with the Electoral Commission's removal of a PKR banner. The banner was not marked with a particular code as required by the election rules. However, in response, Sivarasa's campaign team called a press conference to highlight the duplicity of the Electoral Commission by presenting numerous examples of BN material which were not marked with their code and not taken down.

Proliferation of Polling Stations

A necessary component of every opposition campaign is the monitoring of voters and the counting of ballots. Each contesting candidate can send a "polling agent" to sit with the Electoral Commission representative and a BN counterpart to match would-be voters with their names on the electoral roll. These agents would ensure that a voter's name matched that on the role and that the photo on his or her identity card matched him or her. Once someone had voted, their names would be ticked off so that they could not vote a second time.

A "counting agent" was a candidate's representative who counted the ballots along with the Electoral Commission and a BN counterpart to try to ensure accurate tallying. It is widely assumed that without such opposition party polling agents and counting agents (referred to together as PACA), ballot boxes would be tampered with to the detriment of the non-BN party. However, as was the case in Sivarasa's campaign and many others, opposition parties had difficulty finding enough PACAs for polling day in both 2004 and 2008. Case notes that the government has been increasing the number of polling stations to stretch the opposition's resources so that more counting can occur without opposition observation (Case 2001, p. 49).

Other Electoral Biases

In his analysis of statistics from the Malaysian general elections of 2004, Wong Chin Huat outlines some systematic biases that advantage the BN. The result of these biases, such as through gerrymandering — the last redrawing of constituencies occurred in 2002 — was that "the opposition's voters are so under-represented that the 'worth' of a BN voter is matched only by three DAP voters, seven PAS voters, or 28 Keadilan voters" (2005, p. 317; for a fuller discussion of gerrymandering in Malaysia, see Brown 2005). This pro-BN bias of the electoral system was recapitulated on a smaller scale in the 2008 election results with the BN winning 51.2 per cent of the popular vote but winning 63 per cent of the parliamentary seats.

One of the number of irregularities that occurred on election day of 2004 was that thousands of voters could not find their names on electoral rolls in 17 constituencies (ibid., p. 316). Some constituencies in Malaysia also showed an unusually high number of unreturned ballots "exceeding 10,000 in two constituencies — suggesting instances of ballot stuffing, ballot discarding, or tampering with the numbers" (ibid.).

What is evident in the foregoing observations on Malaysian elections, some of which are echoed in Transparency International's *Global Corruption Report 2008* (2008, pp. 201–205), is that using the electoral system in Malaysia poses a great number of difficulties for those who wish to challenge the status quo. Running as an independent candidate or as a small party may split the protest vote and help to entrench a regime that one may wish to challenge. Joining or supporting an established political party, however, does nothing to diversify the number of voices and viewpoints and one may end up giving apparent weight to an ideology that one does not necessary support. As we have seen, this latter aspect of Malaysian democracy and the first-past-the-post system have resulted in what may well be a false sense of appearance of support for an Islamist agenda which in turn has legitimized the Islamic discourse and seen constitutional freedoms curtailed in the name of Islam.

Consequently, some civil society actors have sought to reform and challenge Malaysia's democratic system. This was particularly evident in the lead up to and during the 2008 elections. Such movements included the Women's Candidacy Initiative and a series of public rallies in 2007.

WOMEN'S CANDIDACY INITIATIVE

The Women's Candidacy Initiative (WCI) is a loose and unregistered movement of Malaysians whose aim is to see greater representation of women in Parliament. WCI also places an emphasis on working independently of established political parties as, in their view, male-dominated party structures prevail in Malaysia and party lines often have the effect of sidelining women and their interests.

To date, WCI has actively participated in two Malaysian elections — in 1999 and 2008. In 1999 WCI put forward Zaitun "Toni" Kasim as a candidate to contest the seat of Selayang in the state of Selangor. In 2008 WCI undertook an inventive and high-profile voter education campaign revolving around the fictional character of Mak Bedah (Aunty Bedah) who publically engaged with candidates on their views on various issues that effected women including the functioning of the electoral system and the sexist behaviour of some parliamentarians.

WCI's beginnings lie in the context of Malaysia's authoritarianism and the difficulty that women's groups experienced in advocating for their agenda. The twelve-year long process required to realize Malaysia's Domestic Violence Act is illustrative of this and symptomatic of the difficulties experienced by women's rights activists generally (see Martinez 2004, pp. 61–63), and indeed, it was a proximal cause of WCI's establishment.

It is worth noting here that probably the most significant sticking point in the Domestic Violence Act was — and continues to be — conservative interpretations of Islam which do not condemn wife-beating and do not recognize a wife's right to refuse sex with her husband and so do not recognize the crime of marital rape. This is illustrated in the comments of the Mufti of Perak, Dr Harussani Zakaria and which were supported by some Syariah lawyers. The Mufti said when the issue of marital rape resurfaced in 2004, that "[a] husband has the right to be intimate with his wife and the wife must obey. If the wife refuses, the rule of 'nusyuz' (disobedient) applies and the husband is not required to provide financial assistance to her" (cited in Kent 2004; parentheses original). The Domestic Violence Act of 1994 can be seen then as not addressing marital rape because domestic violence is "any conduct or act, sexual or otherwise, from which the victim has a right to abstain". Far from having the right to abstain, a Muslim wife, by refusing sex, can be regarded as having been *nusyuz* — sometimes translated as disobedient — which is grounds for divorce.

Identifying the lack of women in Parliament to advocate for women's rights (around 10 per cent since 1999 to the time of writing), the formation of WCI "grew out of the recognition that the political participation of women at every level of decision making is vital to advance and maintain the rights of women and to represent their concerns" (Martinez 2004, p. 80). By having more women in Parliament, the legitimacy of discourses and views that were insensitive or derogatory to women could be more effectively challenged.

WCI in 1999, as in 2008, was made up of women and men, many of whom had connections to the women's movement in Malaysia, but were acting in their individual capacities (see also Martinez 2004, p. 88). In 1999, WCI contested the seat of Selayang. This seat was largely unwanted by any party at the time because the incumbent was a vice-president of the MCA, Chan Kong Choy, who was generally regarded as unbeatable. Although PAS provided some men as bodyguards, and while Toni ran under the banner of the DAP, she and WCI remained independent of both parties. Running on a DAP ticket was largely an administrative convenience because independents are not allotted by the Electoral Commission the symbol which will appear on the voting forms until the first day of campaigning. This gives little time to prepare and print materials and to associate in the public's mind the symbol with the candidate during Malaysia's short campaign period (the extreme brevity of which is regarded by opposition parties and the electoral reform movement, Bersih, as greatly handicapping non-BN parties with poor access to the mainstream media).

Despite participating in Malaysia's electoral system, and so potentially affirming its legitimacy, WCI sought to re-invent the nature of a political campaign. It sought to be sensitive to the needs of women and be considerate of the demands that society tends to place on them and to work around those. Toni recollected to me in 2008 what WCI's 1999 campaign sought to achieve:

> Because women often have multiple duties at home and work, we were flexible with letting people contribute time when they were able to. We weren't hardnosed about it like other political parties who demanded that you gave 150 per cent. And we only got people to do things they were comfortable doing. We didn't make anyone climb poles [to hang flags]. Some women just felt they could run the office, or even just clean it, because that was what they knew how to do. One woman just wanted to give people massages when they needed one because that was what she knew. We gave people the space to contribute in the way they wanted. And in the evening we sat in a circle to talk about how the day went. Of course, the PAS guys told us not to do all this touchy-feely stuff, but we were running a different kind of campaign to the ones they were used to.

Despite losing the contest for Selayang, WCI managed to reduce its opponent's winning margin from 38,627 votes in the 1995 elections, to 8,835 votes in 1999. And, by successfully bringing women's issues to media attention, and by creating a campaign atmosphere conducive to women's participation, members of WCI regarded their campaign a success. WCI did not participate in the 2004 elections for various reasons. While not directly articulated by WCI members in 2008, WCI's non-participation in the 2004 elections probably owed a great deal to the promise of democratization which appeared to accompany the new Prime Ministership of Abdullah Badawi, as well as the personal circumstances of some members. In 2008, however, WCI reformed in view of various factors including increased sexism in Parliament, a remark by Abdullah that, contrary to the Ninth Malaysia Plan, the target of having 30 per cent of Parliament made up of women would be revised down to 20 per cent, and the general failure of his promise for greater government accountability. In the near background were the effects of Islamization described in this book, in particular issues of freedom of religion which numerous WCI members regarded as having a particularly negative impact on women.

Although intending to recreate their 1999 campaign, Toni, who was to again be their candidate, was forced to withdraw four days from the start of the 2008 campaign period owing to an illness that later claimed her life (Lee 2008*c*). Unable to find a suitable candidate at short notice, WCI undertook an innovative voter education campaign revolving around the theatrical character of Mak Bedah. By using playful Youtube videos, blogs, and by publicly engaging almost a dozen candidates from established parties regarding their views on various matters pertaining to women in Malaysia (see Photo 5), WCI drew attention to women's disadvantaged position in Malaysia and to hurdles to women's participation in democracy including, for example, the very high election deposits. WCI's campaign attracted significant media attention including the front pages of local newspapers as well as segments on Al Jazeera news network and Australian radio. While the coverage Mak Bedah managed to get during the elections exceeded WCI members' best expectations, post-election discussions among WCI members have tended to affirm that, as well as advocating for electoral reform between elections, WCI would return to working more directly towards getting women into Parliament as candidates independent of parties during electoral campaign periods.

BERSIH AND THE PUBLIC RALLIES OF 2007

Authors who have sought to understand why the elections on 8 March 2008 yielded such bad results for the BN have all suggested that a number of rallies in Malaysia in late 2007 had a significant impact. These rallies by different groups all publicly sought redress for different perceived injustices.

The first of these demonstrations was organized by the Malaysian Trade Union Congress in June to protest the government's refusal to institute minimum wage legislation (Ooi, Saravanamuttu, and Lee 2008, p. 10). These demonstrations were followed on 26 September by a march organized by the Malaysian Bar Council. Described as a "Walk for Justice" and drawing 2,000 lawyers and other supporters who marched to the Prime Minister's Office in Putrajaya, the Bar Council protested apparent government inaction over video recordings showing a prominent lawyer, V.K. Lingham, apparently informing a judge that he was able to influence judicial appointments.

These demonstrations were dwarfed, however, by two rallies held in November 2007. The second of these, held by the Hindu Rights Action Force (HINDRAF), took place on 25 November. Despite arrests of HINDRAF leaders and roadblocks which prevented many would-be demonstrators from reaching Kuala Lumpur, the site of the rally, some 30,000 to 40,000 Indian ralliers managed to assemble in the city. They sought to show their support for a petition to be submitted to the British Embassy (see also ibid., pp. 11–12). This petition requested that the Queen of England appoint a Queen's Counsel to represent Indian Malaysians in their suit against the British government for, in effect, exploiting them during the colonial period and for not ensuring their welfare when Malaysia gained independence.

While the HINDRAF rally was held ostensibly to support a petition to be delivered to the British Embassy, more and less explicit in the demonstration was a protest against the BN government for overlooking the interests of poor Indians in favour of an emphasis on Malay rights. Having little scope for electoral means of expressing this sentiment, and with HINDRAF being unsuccessful in registering as a political party, a public show of force was one of the few avenues open to such an ethnic minority with little ability to gain representation of their interests in proportion to the size of their community (for reasons related to the first-past-the-post system described earlier).

Indeed, it should be noted that HINDRAF itself came into being in the context of a high-profile example of Islam having apparently undue dominance over the rights of followers of other religions. This incident was the case of M. Moorthy whose corpse was claimed by Muslim authorities against the will of his Hindu wife who knew nothing of his alleged conversion to Islam (see Chapter 6). Thus, in addition to seeking improvements in the socio-economic position of Indians in Malaysia, the HINDRAF movement should be seen in the context of Malay hegemony and a political and legal system which appears to advance the cause of Islam at the expense of the faiths of non-Muslims. The HINDRAF rally in turn should be seen in the context of a democratic system which is unable to subtly reflect voters' desires, thus necessitating other forms of expression.

A few of these defects in the Malaysian electoral system were the focus of another movement known as Bersih (Clean), which culminated in a rally on 10 November. Bersih is a movement involving five opposition parties and 64 politically unaffiliated civil society organizations (Ooi, Saravanamuttu, and Lee 2008, p. 11) that had joined forces to call for electoral reform. The rally on 10 November was in support of a memorandum to be submitted to the Sultan (see Photos 6 and 7).

This memorandum outlined five reforms that Bersih argued would result in cleaner and fairer elections. These reforms were fair access to the media, a clean-up of the electoral roll (whose poor maintenance allegedly enabled multiple and phantom voting), the use of indelible ink on the fingers of those who voted (to prevent multiple voting), the abolition of postal voting for military and police personnel (whose suspiciously high rates of government support appeared to indicate undue interference), a minimum of twenty-one days campaign period, and free and fair access to the mainstream media.

Despite the warnings by the Prime Minister for Malaysians to eschew demonstrations which would threaten stability, and to instead "make their evaluation at the ballot boxes" (Shahanaaz 2007, p. N3), approximately 40,000 ralliers attended the demonstration. Many wore yellow, the colour of the Bersih movement and also of royalty, indicating the role that Bersih saw the Sultan playing in realizing democratic reform.

While the demonstration was ostensibly intended to gather at Dataran Merdeka (Independence Square) in Kuala Lumpur, owing to a police block-ade of that point, four alternative gathering points were publicized shortly before the rally. Falsely advertising Dataran Merdeka as the gathering point may always have been a ploy to dilute police forces (Ooi, Saravanamuttu, and Lee 2008, p. 45). From the four points the ralliers moved independently toward the Sultan's palace which constituted the final assembly point. Unlike the HINDRAF rally which saw a severe police crackdown includ-ing some ISA arrests (ibid., pp. 11–12), the Bersih rally saw 34 people arrested and water-cannon and tear-gas use at just one of the four meeting points. Also, unlike the HINDRAF rally which was prominently and negatively portrayed on the front page of the newspapers the following day (see Photo 8), the coverage of the Bersih rally was conspicuous by its almost complete absence of representation in the media.[2]

Despite being condemned by the government, the Bersih rally was not completely ignored by the Electoral Commission. The campaign period for the 2008 election was extended to thirteen days (up from eight in 2004) and indelible ink was purchased for use. However, prior to the election, the forecast use of the ink was rescinded on the grounds that the police had claimed that indelible ink had been smuggled in by elements wishing to cause confusion and mischief during the elections. The Home Minister, Syed Hamid Albar, admitted after the elections that there was in fact no evidence of this (Beh and Rahman 2008).

THE END OF RACIAL POLITICS?

Despite the significant public displays of discontent, and despite some reforms to the electoral system in response to the Bersih rally, the results of the 2008 elections surprised everybody. A number of high-profile BN candidates lost seats that were previously regarded as safe and a number of opposition party candidates, including Sivarasa, finally tasted victory (see Photo 9). The biggest winner among the opposition parties was PKR, which won thirty-one out of the ninety-seven parliamentary seats it contested. This was followed by the DAP which won twenty-eight of the forty-seven parliamentary seats it contested and PAS which mustered twenty-three of sixty-six (for a fuller discussion of the results, see Ooi, Saravanamuttu, and Lee 2008).

While the leader of PKR, Anwar Ibrahim, has claimed that the cancellation of the use of indelible ink cost the opposition as many as fifteen seats, the results of the 2008 elections, which deprived the BN of its two-thirds majority in Parliament and saw five states into opposition party control, was largely regarded as a victory for the opposition parties. Commentators have described the results as a "political tsunami" and, most pertinently, as indicating the demise of "race-based" politics. For example, Abdul Rashid Moten writes that "[m]any Malaysians voted for the opposition by crossing ethnic boundaries. Evidently, there is a change in the behaviour of the Malaysian electorate towards multiculturalism" (2009, p. 40).

While Lee Hock Guan (in Ooi, Saravanamuttu, and Lee 2008, pp. 80–121) has shown there were high rates of voters voting for candidates not from their own background, the conclusion that this indicates the end of racial politics or a move towards multiculturalism does not follow. Where a voter has only a choice between so few candidates as in Malaysia's first-past-the-post system, the ability for that vote to reflect anything about the voter's views is so poor as to be effectively uninterpretable. Furthermore, as

Lee Hock Guan notes, the high rates of cross-ethnic voting were observed principally in highly urbanized Kuala Lumpur and Selangor, while "the old ethnic voting pattern continued to prevail in the multi-ethnic states of Pahang, Malacca, Negeri Sembilan, and especially Johor" (in ibid., p. 113). As Malay-dominated states were contested by Malay-dominated parties, cross-ethnic voting naturally could not be measured there. While so much of the electioneering and regular politicking outside of campaign periods continues to affirm the salience of race and religion, it cannot be concluded that the end of ethnic politics is nigh, or that Islam or the Islamic state issue has been permanently put to rest despite PAS's soft-peddling of it before and after the 2008 elections.

Notes

1. This and subsequent conversions of currency from Malaysian ringgit to U.S. dollars were correct in February 2010.
2. Only the Kuala Lumpur and Selangor paper *Sinar* gave the Bersih rally front page coverage. *The Star* and the *New Straits Times*, for example, ran only small articles in their inner pages and referred largely to the traffic inconvenience caused by the rally.

Conclusion

ISLAM, DEMOCRACY, AND ACTIVISM IN MALAYSIA

Malaysian Islam made headlines around the world in late 2008 when the National Fatwa Council of Malaysia, which composes *fatwas* that may be adopted and enforced by individual states, announced first that it was *haram* (forbidden) for Muslim women to behave like tomboys and, second, that it was against Islam to practise yoga while chanting mantras. While the BBC was able to make light of the "tomboy *fatwa*", describing it as a *fatwa* against women wearing trousers, what is apparent is that there is a willingness on the part of Islamic bodies of the Malaysian State to seek to control the minutiae of people's lives.

Any hopes that Islamization would be halted by what many regarded as an electoral shift away from ethno-religious politics in the 2008 elections are unlikely to remain strong in the face of these *fatwas* and the other developments. Other examples of deference to conservative Islamic sensibilities include the pop singer Rihanna agreeing in the face of Islamists' protests in January 2009 to dress more conservatively on stage than she otherwise would have, and the shows of Inul Daratista of Indonesia, who performs a gyrating dance to music known as *dangdut*, repeatedly being cancelled and rescheduled owing to official protests from Islamists from both PAS and UMNO over the sexual nature of her performances.

The ascent and current place of a general Islamic consciousness in Malaysia is significant and pervasive. A number of Malaysians lamented to me that there was an obsession in Malaysia for every aspect of life to require the stamp of approval from Islamic authorities. One lawyer felt that the silliest and most telling example of this was the trend to find even on bottles of mineral water the symbol for *halal* (permissible) certification from the Jabatan Kemajuan Islam Malaysia (Department of Islamic Development Malaysia, JAKIM). On another occasion, members of Sisters in Islam have described to me the trend for departments such as the Department for Women, Family and Community Development to send policies to JAKIM for vetting and approval even though there was no need for this to occur and that JAKIM does not request to vet policies. A final example worth noting is that prior to the 2008 elections, the Electoral Commission deemed it necessary to get approval from the National Fatwa Council for the use of indelible ink.

There may, however, be signs that the deference towards Islamic authority is changing. While it is difficult to measure how deep this inclination goes, the outcry over the yoga *fatwa* in particular is noteworthy. A great deal of media attention was paid to the many who publicly challenged the notion that yoga was in any way contrary to Islamic dictates. While yoga does have roots in Hinduism, it is frequently nowadays practised by individuals of all religions and without much trace of its Hindu origins, and those who protested pointed out the National Fatwa Council's ignorance of this. Although it was true that the *fatwa* had stressed that yoga was forbidden if conducted while chanting mantras, the stain of the *fatwa* on yoga was felt to be more general. Furthermore, the National Fatwa Council chairman, Datuk Dr Abdul Shukor Husin, had stated that "doing yoga, even just the physical movements, is a step towards erosion of one's faith in the religion, hence Muslims should avoid it" (in Mazwin 2008). Part of the protest even included an open demonstration of yoga on 22 December 2008 by a Malay yoga practitioner. This demonstration, held in Kuala Lumpur, sought to demonstrate both that yoga does not conflict with Islamic dictates and that the National Fatwa Council had issued the *fatwa* in ignorance of the way yoga was in fact practised in Malaysia (i.e. without mantras).

The extensive permeation of religious authority into the realms of everyday life, especially when this authority issues firm rulings on relatively minor matters, is what is described by Roy Rappaport as "oversanctification". Rappaport proposes that all religions have, at their heights of sanctity, Ultimate Sacred Postulates. These Postulates are unspecific with regard to material obligations. Examples include the Jewish *Shema* and the Islamic *Kalimat al Shahada* (the latter of which translates as, "I testify that there is no god but One God, and I testify that Mohammed is his prophet"

(Rappaport 1999, p. 277)). It is their non-specificity that allows personal meaning and reverence to be invested in Ultimate Sacred Postulates and which makes them so broadly acceptable.

Lower in sanctity, according to Rappaport, are cosmological axioms. These "refer to assumptions concerning the fundamental structure of the universe or, to put it differently ... refer to the paradigmatic relationships in accordance with which the cosmos is constructed" (ibid., p. 264). Lower again on the scale of sanctity are rules which are more specific as to people's conduct. These rules are subject to evolution in the face of necessity. The transgression or changing of these rules does not invalidate the Ultimate Sacred Postulates that lend sanctity to both them and cosmological axioms.

According to Rappaport, rules may, however, become "oversanctified". As an example of oversanctification he cites Pope Paul IV's encyclical in 1969 which elevated the Catholic Church's rules on birth control to a level of sanctity equivalent to other doctrines such as the Immaculate Conception. Rappaport notes that this led to the widespread defection of Catholics from the religion. Many of those who remained were also "less likely to acquiesce routinely to Vatican dicta on social matters of any sort" (ibid., p. 440; for a similar controversy in 2009, see Butt and Hooper 2009).

A similar reaction with regard to Islam can be seen in responses to the yoga *fatwa* (as the final straw). Zainah Anwar expressed such a view during a discussion in which we both participated in 2008.

> The more Islam is in the public sphere, the more people will challenge the authorities that speak in the name of Islam. Because before it didn't impact on you so much. [Now that] it interferes in the private choices of citizens [they] will contest this interpretation of Islam. So, like with the yoga fatwa, what they [the National Fatwa Council] are saying yoga's impact is, and that this is *haram*, doesn't fit with what we're experiencing when we practise yoga. And that is where the questioning of authority comes in. And the public outrage, which is new. Before people would just hide and feel guilty. Not anymore. I really feel in the end that it is they who are going to become irrelevant.

However, a number of caveats are in order before concluding that there may be a widespread diminution of Malaysian Muslims' deference towards Islamic authority. One is that the outcry over the yoga *fatwa* is not the first public outcry over the conduct of Islamic authorities. In Chapter 6, I described the public condemnation of the Zouk raid conducted in Kuala Lumpur in 2005. It is worth pointing out that what the Zouk raid and the yoga *fatwa* share is that both affected urban middle-class Malaysians. The practices of both nightclubbing and yoga are ones that predominate among urban middle- and upper-class Malaysians who are better able to articulate their objections and to not be cowed by authority. Furthermore, as noted to me by one activist, tan beng hui, this outcry also appeared to receive the endorsement of the Sultan of Selangor who said that future *fatwa*s that pertain to "issues involving the general public" should be approved by the Sultans "to avoid any confusion and controversy" (Associated Press 2008). Without such royal support restraining the potential for the deployment of coercion, it is uncertain whether the protests would have been as vigorous or as well-reported in the media.

What Rappaport's insight into oversanctification tells us, and what the public reaction during instances such as the yoga *fatwa* and the Zouk raid reveal, is the potential for Islamization to undermine the very structures of authority on which it rests. If an authority asserts the divinity of certain rules or precepts, and if society cannot bring itself to abide by them, the legitimacy of that authority is at risk of being rejected or ignored along with those rules. At worst, according to Rappaport, extending such high levels of sanctity to everyday specifics unnecessarily ossifies aspects of life that should be able to evolve and that ossification weakens a society's ability to cope with inevitable change (1999, pp. 443–44).

The above, however, does not mean that deference to Islamic authority and Islamization will inevitably wane in the future. The vagaries of innumerable local and global contingencies make predictions regarding this well nigh impossible. What can be concluded from the foregoing in this book is that individuals, and democracy more generally, rely on the presence of an array of different discourses and realms of action within which to advocate for what they regard as justice. Particularly important is when such realms, when found to be ineffectual on their own, are brought together to try to improve the efficacy of advocacy. This is what was apparent in the *Article 11* coalition, as well as with Bersih and the Women's Candidacy Initiative. By combining spaces, whether it is the law, activism, Islam, or elections, they improved and widened the space in which civil society could operate in Malaysia and improved the efficacy of the discourses they deployed.

Competing discourses, however, do not just contest each others' logical conclusions, with the most rational winning out. Such is evident in the tortured judgements of the courts in the cases of Lina Joy and Shamala Sathiyaseelan described in Chapters 4 and 6. It is with the apparent weight of public opinion that a discourse's interpretation into action and its public legitimacy rise and fall, with real effects on people. A discourse — be it Islam or constitutionalism — or a realm of action — be it legal or electoral — will also be fraught with pros and cons. Contesting the status quo by taking part in elections may confirm the legitimacy of a bad or corrupt electoral structure. Undertaking a legal challenge in the courts likewise affirms the courts' legitimacy and risks creating an unwanted legal precedent which will worsen the prospects for future legal challenges.

While each method of engagement will have its attendant dilemmas associated with it, what remains important in all cases is the legitimacy of diversity of opinion. This does not mean to say all opinions are equally valid. What it does mean to say is that opinions and viewpoints should succeed or fail on the grounds of support or otherwise after comparison and rebuttal. Opinions and viewpoints should not be ruled out merely because they contradict consensus or because they come from allegedly unqualified quarters.

Measuring the support or otherwise of opinions and viewpoints of course requires a mechanism capable of doing this. Such mechanisms are largely absent in Malaysia. The electoral system, as I have described in the previous chapter, cannot be interpreted as being able to reflect the people's will. Other forms of democratic engagement are greatly constrained — as in the case of the media — or liable to coercive suppression — as in the case of public demonstrations. While authoritarianism does not require the cloak of any religion, the conservative politicized Islam that often prevails in Malaysia adds a further layer of sanctity which complicates the advocacy initiatives of many activists. Observers of Malaysia and its Islam should not conclude that Islam per se is necessarily as conservative or restrictive as it often is there, but that Malaysia's Islam is greatly conditioned by the local conditions in which it arose including, for example, Malaysia's electoral system. And, as this book also demonstrates, it is also subject to significant and diverse challenges.

BIBLIOGRAPHY

Abdul Kadir Sulaiman. "Md Hakim Lee v Majlis Agama Islam Wilayah Persekutuan, Kuala Lumpur". *Malaysian Law Journal*, no. 1 (1998): 681–89.

Abdullah Badawi. "Moving Forward — Towards Excellence". *New Straits Times*, 24 September 2004, p. 12.

Abraham, Collin E.R. *The Naked Social Order: The Roots of Racial Polarisation in Malaysia*. Subang Jaya: Pelanduk, 2005.

Abu-Lughod, Lila. "The Romance of Resistance: Tracing Transformations of Power Through Bedouin Women". *American Ethnologist* 17, no. 1 (1990): 41–55.

Adabi, Al-Mansor. "Ahmad Ibrahim in the Service of Islam". In *Malaysian Legal Essays: A Collection of Essays in Honour of Professor Emeritus Datuk Ahmad Ibrahim*, edited by M. B. Hooker. Kuala Lumpur: Malaysian Law Journal, 1986.

Ahmad Ibrahim. *The Administration of Islamic Law in Malaysia*. Kuala Lumpur: Institute of Islamic Understanding, 2000.

Albrecht, Holger. "How Can Opposition Support Authoritarianism? Lessons from Egypt". *Democratization* 12, no. 3 (2005): 378–97.

Allport, Gordon Willard. "The Functional Autonomy of Motives". *The American Journal of Psychology* 15, no. 1/4 (1937): 141–56.

Anuar, Mustapha K. "Defining Democratic Discourses: The Mainstream Press". In *Democracy in Malaysia: Discourses and Practices*, edited by Francis Loh Kok Wah and Khoo Boo Teik. Richmond: Curzon, 2002.

Arfa'eza A. Aziz and Nurul Nazirin. "Jawi raid 'un-Islamic', says Sisters in Islam". *Malaysiakini.com*, 2 February 2005. <http://www.malaysiakini.com/news/33341>. Accessed 2 February, 2005.

Armstrong, Karen. *Muhammad: A Biography of the Prophet*. New York: Harper Collins, 1993.

———. *Islam: A Short Introduction*. New York: Modern Library, 2002.

———. "Contesting what is Sacred". *The Age*, 20 March 2006. <http://www.theage.com.au/news/opinion/contesting-what-is-sacred/2006/03/19/11427032 11883.html?page=fullpage>. Accessed 3 October 2006.

Asad, Talal. "Ethnography, Literature, and Politics: Some Readings and Uses of Salman Rushdie's The Satanic Verses". *Cultural Anthropology* 5, no. 3 (1990): 239–69.

Associated Press. "Fatwa on Yoga: Malay royal questions ban on yoga for Muslims". *Jakarta Post*, 24 November 2008. <http://www.thejakartapost.com/news/2008/11/24/malay-royal-questions-ban-yoga-muslims.html>. Accessed 3 April 2009.

Bari, Abdul Aziz. "Issues in Islamisation of Law in Malaysia". Paper presented at the International Conference on Harmonisation of Shariah and Civil Law, Kuala Lumpur, Malaysia, 20–21 October 2003.

Bari, Abdul Aziz and Farid Sufian Shuaib. *Constitution of Malaysia: Text and Commentary*. Petaling Jaya: Prentice Hall, 2004.

Beh Lih Yi and Rahman Ghazali. "No evidence of indelible ink smugglers". *Malaysiakini.com*, 6 May 2008. <http://malaysiakini.com/news/82394>. Accessed 3 April 2009.

Bell, Daniel A. "Which Rights are Universal?". *Political Theory* 27, no. 6 (1999): 849–56.

Blais, Andre. "The Debate over Electoral Systems". *International Political Science Review* 12, no. 3 (1991): 239–60.

Bon, Edmund. "Bersih gathering: Of facts and violations". In *The Malaysian Bar*, November 2007. <http://www.malaysianbar.org.my/human_rights/bersih_gathering_of_facts_and_violations.html>. Accessed 1 April 2009.

Bougarel, Xavier. "The Role of Balkan Muslims in Building a European Islam. EPC Issue". *European Policy Centre (EPC) Issue Paper*, no. 43 (2005).

Boyer, Pascal. *Religion Explained: The Human Instincts that Fashion Gods, Spirits and Ancestors*. London: Vintage, 2002.

Brown, Gordon K. "The Enemy of My Enemy? Opposition Parties during the Mahathir Years". In *Reflections: The Mahathir Years*, edited by Bridget Welsh. Washington: Southeast Asia Studies, Johns Hopkins University-SAIS, 2004.

————. "Playing the (Non)Ethnic Card: The Electoral System and Ethnic Voting Patterns in Malaysia". *Ethnopolitics* 44, no. 4 (2005): 429–45.

Bunce, Valerie. "Rethinking Recent Democratization: Lessons from the Postcommunist Experience". *World Politics* 55, no. 2 (2003): 167–94.

Butt, Riazat and John Hooper. "Vatican intervenes to calm escalating storm over Pope's comments on HIV and condoms". *The Guardian*, 19 March 2009, p. 18.

Carr, John E. and Tan Eng Kong. "In Search of the True Amok: Amok as Viewed Within the Malay Culture". *American Journal of Psychiatry* 133, no. 11 (1976): 1295–99.

Case, William. "Malaysia's Resilient Pseudodemocracy". *Journal of Democracy* 12, no. 1 (2001): 43–57.

————. "Southeast Asia's Hybrid Regimes: When Do Voters Change Them?". *Journal of East Asian Studies* 5, no. 2 (2005): 215–37.

Castoriadis, Cornelius. *World in Fragments: Writings on Politics, Society, Psychoanalysis, and the Imagination*. Stanford: Stanford University Press, 1997*a*.

————. *The Castoriadis Reader*. Translated and edited by David Ames Curtis. Oxford: Blackwell, 1997*b*.

Cheah Boon Keng. "Politics". In *The Shaping of Malaysia*, edited by Amarjit Kaur and Ian Metcalfe. London: Macmillan Press, 1999.

————. *Malaysia: The Making of a Nation.* Singapore: Institute of Southeast Asian Studies, 2002.

Christian Federation of Malaysia. "Govt: M'sia is an Islamic State". *Catholic Asian News* (March 2002), pp. 10–11.

Colas, Dominique. *Civil Society and Fanaticism: Conjoined Histories.* Stanford: Stanford University Press, 1997.

Comaroff, John L. and Jean Comaroff. "Introduction". In *Civil Society and the Political Imagination in Africa*, edited by John L. Comaroff and Jean Comaroff. Chicago: The University of Chicago Press, 1999.

Darshini, Shamini. "Religious snoop squad comes under fire". *The New Straits Times*, 18 January 2006, p. 4.

Davidson, Ryan. "Jawi affair a Muslim issue". *Malaysiakini.com*, 7 February 2005. <http://www.malaysiakini.com/letters/33462>. Accessed 3 October 2006.

Dorraj, Manochehr. "The Crisis of Modernity and Religious Revivalism: A Comparative Study of Islamic Fundamentalism, Jewish Fundamentalism and Liberation Theology". *Social Compass* 46, no. 2 (1999): 225–40.

Edwards, Audrey. "Huge turnout at ISA debate as Nazri and Lim battle it out". *The Star*, 27 July 2004. <http://thestar.com.my/news/story.asp?file=/2004/7/27/nation/8530116&sec=nation>. Accessed 3 October 2006.

El-Affendi, Abdelwahab. *Who Needs An Islamic State?* 2nd ed. London: Malaysia Think Tank, 2008.

el-Gaili, Ahmad T. "Federalism and the Tyranny of Religious Majorities: Challenges to Islamic Fundamentalism in Sudan". *Harvard International Law Journal* 45, no. 2 (2004): 503–46.

Esman, Milton. J. *Ethnic Politics.* Ithaca: Cambridge University Press, 1994.

Faaland, Just, Jack Parkinson, and Rais Saniman. *Growth and Ethnic Inequality: Malaysia's New Economic Policy.* London: Hurst and Company, 1990.

Faiza Tamby Chik J. "Majlis Ugama Islam Pulau Pinang dan Seberang Perai lwn Shaik Zolkaffily bin Shaik Natar dan lain-lain". *Malaysian Law Journal*, no. 4 (2002): 130–38.

————. "Lina Joy v Majlis Agama Islam Wilayah & Anor". *Malaysian Law Journal*, no. 2 (2004): 119–44.

Farmer, Paul. "Sidney W. Mintz Lecture for 2001: An Anthropology of Structural Violence". *Current Anthropology* 45, no. 3 (2004): 305–25.

Fauwaz Abdul Aziz. "Don't stir the hornet's nest called Malay rights". *Malaysiakini.com*, 24 September 2004. <http://www.malaysiakini.com/news/30305>. Accessed 13 June 2006.

————. "Groups want commission to review all civil, Islamic laws". *Malaysiakini. com*, 22 March 2005. <http://www.malaysiakini.com/news/34647>. Accessed 3 October 2006.

————. "Muslim coalition submits 700,000 signatures". *Malaysiakini.com*, 29 September 2006. <http://www.malaysiakini.com/news/57511>. Accessed 30 September 2006.

Fenton, Steve. "Malaysia and Capitalist Modernisation: Plural and Multicultural Models". *International Journal of Multicultural Studies* 5, no. 2 (2003): 137–49.

Fernando, Joseph M. *The Making of the Malayan Constitution*. Kuala Lumpur: The Malaysian Branch of the Royal Asiatic Society, 2002.

Firth, Raymond. *Religion: A Humanist Interpretation*. London: Routledge, 1996.

Foley, Rebecca A. "Muslim Women's Challenges to Islamic Law: The Case of Malaysia". *International Feminist Journal of Politics* 6, no. 1 (2004): 53–84.

Fraser, Nancy. "Rethinking the Public Sphere: A Contribution to the Critique of Actually Existing Democracy". *Social Text*, no. 25/26 (1990): 56–80.

Fritz, Nicole and Martin Flaherty. "Unjust Order: Malaysia's Internal Security Act". *Fordham International Law Journal* 26, no. 5 (2003): 1345–437.

Funston, John. *Malay Politics in Malaysia: A Study of the United Malays National Organisation and Party Islam*. Kuala Lumpur: Heinemann Educational Books (Asia), 1980.

Gardiner, Michael E. "Wild publics and grotesque symposiums: Habermas and Bakhtin on dialogue, everyday life and the public sphere". *The Sociological Review* 52, no. 1 (2004): 28–48.

Gatsiounis, Ioannis. "Malaysia, 'too sensitive' for debate". *Asia Times Online*, 4 August 2006. <http://www.atimes.com/atimes/Southeast_Asia/HH04Ae01.html>. Accessed 3 October 2006.

Geertz, Clifford. *The Interpretation of Cultures: Selected Essays by Clifford Geertz*. New York: Basic Books, 1973.

Gilner, Salvador. "Civil Society and its Future". In *Civil Society: Theory, History and Comparison*, edited by John A. Hall. Cambridge: Polity Press, 1995.

Gilsenan, Michael. *Recognizing Islam: Religion and Society in the Modern Middle East*. Rev. ed. London: I.B. Taurus, 2000.

Gomes, Alberto. "Peoples and Cultures". In *The Shaping of Malaysia*, edited by Amarjit Kaur and Ian Metcalfe. London: Macmillan Press, 1999.

Habermas, Jürgen. *The Structural Transformation of the Public Sphere: An Inquiry into a Category of Bourgeois Society*. Translated by Thomas Burger with Frederick Lawrence. Cambridge: MIT Press, 1992.

Hall, John A. "In Search of Civil Society". In *Civil Society: Theory, History and Comparison*, edited by John A. Hall. Cambridge: Polity Press, 1995.

Hann, Chris. "Introduction: Political society and civil anthropology". In *Civil society: Challenging western models*, edited by Chris Hann and Elizabeth Dunn. London: Routledge, 1996.

Hatta, S. Mohamed. "A Malay crosscultural worldview and forensic review of amok". *Australian and New Zealand Journal of Psychiatry* 30, no. 4 (1996): 505–10.

Hefner, Robert W. "Introduction: Multiculturalism and Citizenship in Malaysia, Singapore and Indonesia". In *The Politics of Multiculturalism: Pluralism and*

Citizenship in Malaysia, Singapore and Indonesia, edited by Robert W. Hefner. Honolulu: University of Hawai'i Press, 2001.

———. "Introduction: Modernity and the Remaking of Muslim Politics". In *Remaking Muslim Politics: Pluralism, Contestation, Democracy*, edited by Robert W. Hefner. Princeton: Princeton University Press, 2005.

Hegel, Georg Wilhelm Friedrich. *Political Writings*, edited by Laurence Dickey and H.B. Nisbet, translated by H.B. Nisbet. Cambridge: Cambridge University Press, 1999.

Hibbard, Scott W. and David Little. *Islamic Activism and U.S. Foreign Policy*. Washington: United States Institute of Peace Press, 1997.

Hitchens, Christopher. "Giving up on Freedom". *The Age*, 16 February 2006. <http://www.theage.com.au/news/opinion/giving-up-on-freedom/2006/02/15/1139890803075.html>. Accessed 3 October 2006.

Hooker, M.B. "Introduction — Islamic and Malaysian Law: The Contribution of Professor Ahmad Ibrahim". In *Malaysian Legal Essays: A Collection of Essays in Honour of Professor Emeritus Datuk Ahmad Ibrahim*, edited by M.B. Hooker. Kuala Lumpur: Malaysian Law Journal, 1986.

Hooker, Virginia Matheson. *Writing a New Society: Social Change Through the Novel in Malay*. Sydney: Allen and Unwin, 2000.

Hudson, Wayne. "Problematizing European Theories of Civil Society". In *Civil Society in Asia*, edited by David C. Schak and Wayne Hudson. Hampshire: Ashgate, 2003.

Hughes, Tom Eames. *Tangled Worlds: The Story of Maria Hertogh*. Singapore: Institute of Southeast Asian Studies, 1980.

Husna Yusop. "Social science scholars in a quandary". *The Sun*, 8 August 2006. <http://www.sun2surf.com/article.cfm?id=15037>. Accessed 10 September 2006.

Huzir Sulaiman. *Eight Plays*. Kuala Lumpur: Silverfish Books, 2002.

Jackson, Michael D. "Thinking Through the Body: An Essay on Understanding Metaphor". *Social Analysis* X, no. 14 (1983): 127–48.

———. *The Politics of Storytelling: Violence, Transgression and Intersubjectivity*. Copenhagen: Museum Tusculanum Press, 2002.

Jomo Kwame Sundaram. *Growth and Structural Change in the Malaysian Economy*. London: Macmillan, 1990*a*.

———. "Whither Malaysia's New Economic Policy?". *Pacific Affairs* 63, no. 4 (1990*b*): 469–99.

Kamali, Mohammad Hashim. *Punishment in Islamic Law: An Enquiry into the Hudud Bill of Kelantan*. Kuala Lumpur: Ilmiah Publishers, 1995.

———. "Harmonisation of *Shari'ah* and Civil Laws: The Framework and *Modus Operandi*". *IIUM Law Journal* 11, no. 2 (2003*a*): 149–68.

———. "*Shariah* and Civil Law: Towards a Methodology of Harmonisation". Paper presented at the International Conference on Harmonisation of Shariah and Civil Law, Kuala Lumpur, Malaysia, 20–21 October 2003*b*.

Kamarulnizam Abdullah. *The Politics of Islam in Contemporary Malaysia.* Bangi: Penerbit Universiti Kebangsaan Malaysia, 2003.

Kairos. *Doing the Right Thing: A Practical Guide on Legal Matters for Churches in Malaysia.* Petaling Jaya: Kairos Research Centre, 2004.

Kent, Jonathan. "Marital rape law provokes storm". In *BBC News,* 23 August 2004. <http://news.bbc.co.uk/1/hi/world/asia-pacific/3592740.stm>. Accessed 3 April 2009.

———. "Malaysia club raid sparks row". *BBC News,* 18 February 2005. <http://news.bbc.co.uk/1/hi/world/asia-pacific/4276077.stm>. Accessed 3 October 2006.

Khan, Shahnaz. "*Zina* and the moral regulation of Pakistani women". *Feminist Review,* no. 75 (2003): 75–100.

Kon, Yan. "Amok". *British Journal of Psychiatry* 165, no. 5 (1994): 685–89.

Kua Kia Soong. *The Malaysian Civil Rights Movement.* Petaling Jaya: Strategic Information Research Development, 2005.

———. "Racial conflict in Malaysia: Against the official history". *Race & Class* 49, no. 3 (2008): 33–53.

Lane, David. *Leninism: A Sociological Interpretation.* Cambridge: Cambridge University Press, 1981.

Langman, Lauren. "The Dialectic of Unenlightenment: Toward a Critical Theory of Islamic Fundamentalism". *Critical Sociology* 31, no. 1–2 (2005): 243–79.

Latheefa Koya. "Bar Council being retrogressive". *Malaysiakini.com,* 30 August 2001. <http://www.malaysiakini.com/letter/2001/08/2001083008.php>. Accessed 30 August 2001.

Layish, Aharon. "The Transformation of the *Shari'a* from Jurists' Law to Statutory Law in the Contemporary Muslim World". *Die Welt des Islams* 44, no. 1 (2004): 85–113.

Lee, Julian C.H. 2005. "The Narrative Imperative". *Anthropological Forum* 15, no. 2 (2005): 115–30.

———. "Barisan Nasional — Political Dominance and the General Elections of 2004 in Malaysia". *Südostasien Aktuell* 2 (2007): 38–65.

———. "The Fruits of Weeds: Taking Justice at the Commemoration of the Twentieth Anniversary of *Operasi Lalang* in Malaysia". *The Round Table* 97, no. 397 (2008*a*): 605–15.

———. "Batman, Gandhi and Democracy: A Closer Look into the Bar Council Conversion Forum". *Project Malaysia* 1, 2008*b*. <http://www.projectmalaysia. org/2008/09/batman-gandhi-and-democracy-a-closer-look-into-the-bar-council-conversion-forum/>. Accessed 2 April 2009.

———. "Zaitun Kasim, 1967–2008: Malaysian activist". *Off The Edge* 43 (2008*c*): 10–11.

Lim Kit Siang. "EC Chairman Rashid should implement 'caretaker govt' concept to ensure free, fair, clean election". In *Lim Kit Siang for Malaysia,* January 2008. <http://blog.limkitsiang.com/2008/01/06/media-statement-by-parliamentary-

opposition-leader-and-dap-mp-for-ipoh-timur-lim-kit-siang-in-ipoh-on-sunday-6th-january-2008/>. Accessed 3 April 2009.

Linde-Laursen, Anders. "Is something rotten in the state of Denmark? The Muhammad cartoons and Danish political culture". *Contemporary Islam* 1, no. 3 (2007): 265–74.

Lopez, Leslie. "Takeover of newspaper not political, says Berjaya boss". *AsiaMedia: Media News Daily*, 30 January 2008. <http://www.asiamedia.ucla.edu/article-southeastasia.asp?parentid=86397>. Accessed 13 March 2008.

Lunsing, Wim. "Islam versus homosexuality? Some reflections on the assassination of Pim Fortuyn". *Anthropology Today* 19, no. 2 (2003): 19–21.

Luther, Peter. "Review of The literature of the law: A thoughtful entertainment for lawyers and others". *Web Journal of Current Legal Issues*, no. 5 (1998). <http://webjcli.ncl.ac.uk/1998/issue5/luther5.html>. Accessed 13 October 2006.

Mahathir bin Mohamad. *A New Deal for Asia*. Subang Jaya: Pelanduk Publications, 1999.

Malaysiakini.com. "FT PAS Youth defends 'bold' Jawi". *Malaysiakini.com*, 1 February 2005*a*. <http://www.malaysiakini.com/news/33306>. Accessed 3 October 2006.

———. "Tussle over religion of deceased Everest hero". *Malaysiakini.com*, 22 December 2005*b*. <http://www.malaysiakini.com/news/ 44889>. Accessed 16 April 2006.

———. "Everest hero: High Court has no jurisdiction". *Malaysiakini.com*, 28 December 2005*c*. <http://www.malaysiakini.com/news/ 45050>. Accessed 16 April 2006.

———. "PAS 'hypocritical' in demanding ban on SIS". *Malaysiakini.com*, 19 April 2005*d*. <http://www.malaysiakini.com/news/35465>. Accessed 3 October 2006.

———. "Abim wants religious unit in police force". *Malaysiakini.com*, 17 May 2005*e*. <http://www.malaysiakini.com/news/36185>. Accessed 3 October 2006.

———. "Brutal end to anti-fuel hike demo". *Malaysiakini.com*, 28 May 2006. <http://www.malaysiakini.com/news/51684>. Accessed 3 October 2006.

———. "Special report: The Hindraf Protest". *Malaysiakini.com*, 27 November 2007. <http://www.malaysiakini.com/news/75315>. Accessed 28 November 2007.

Malaysian Bar. "Walk for Justice: 'When lawyers walk, something must be very wrong'". *Malaysianbar.org.my*, 26 September 2007. <http://www.malaysianbar.org.my/bar_news/berita_badan_peguam/walk_for_justice_when_lawyers_walk_something_must_be_very_wrong_.html>. Accessed 15 March 2008.

Mandel, Sumit. K. "Boundaries and Beyond: Whither the Cultural Bases of Political Community in Malaysia?". In *The Politics of Multiculturalism: Pluralism and Citizenship in Malaysia, Singapore, and Indonesia*, edited by Robert W. Hefner. Honolulu: University of Hawai'i Press, 2001.

Mansur, Salim. "Muslims, Democracy, and the American Experience". *Middle East Quarterly* 12, no. 3 (2005): 67–75.

Marhalim Abas. "Woman Among 14 Detained". *The Malay Mail*, 19 April 2002, p. 2.

Martinez, Patricia. "Mahathir, Islam, and the New Malay Dilemma". In *Mahathir's Administration: Performance and Crisis in Governance*, edited by Ho Khai Leong and James Chin. Singapore: Times Books International, 2001.

———. "Islam, Constitutional Democracy, and the Islamic State in Malaysia". In *Civil Society in Southeast Asia*, edited by Lee Hock Guan. Singapore: Institute of Southeast Asian Studies, 2004.

———. "Is it always Islam versus civil society?". In *Islam in Southeast Asia: Political, Social and Strategic Challenges for the 21ˢᵗ Century*, edited by K.S. Nathan and M.H. Kamali. Singapore: Institute of Southeast Asian Studies, 2005.

———. *Muslim Identities Public Opinion Survey, Peninsular Malaysia*. Kuala Lumpur: Asia-Europe Institute, University of Malaya, 2006.

Marx, Karl. "The Alleged Split in the International". In *The Thought of Karl Marx: An Introduction*, edited by David McLellan. London: Macmillan, 1971.

Mauzy, Diane K. and Milne, R.S. "The Mahathir Administration in Malaysia: Discipline through Islam". *Pacific Affairs* 56, no. 4 (1983–1984): 617–48.

Mazwin Nik Anis. "Fatwa Council deems ancient form of exercise from India 'haram' for Muslims". *The Star*, 23 November 2008. <http://thestar.com.my/news/story.asp?file=/2008/11/23/nation/2626876&sec=nation>. Accessed 3 April 2009.

McLellan, David. *The Thought of Karl Marx: An Introduction*. London: Macmillan, 1971.

Means, Gordon P. "The Role of Islam in the Political Development of Malaysia". *Comparative Politics* 1, no. 2 (1969): 264–84.

Mehmet, Ozay. *Islamic identity and development: Studies of the Islamic Periphery*. Kuala Lumpur: Forum, 1990.

Merleau-Ponty, Maurice. *Adventures of the Dialectic*. Translated by Joseph Bien. London: Heinemann, 1955.

———. *Humanism and Terror: An Essay on the Communist Problem*. Translated by John O'Neill. Boston: Beacon Press, 1969.

Mernissi, Fatima. *The Veil and the Male Elite: A Feminist Interpretation of Women's Rights in Islam*. Translated by Mary Jo Lakeland. Cambridge: Perseus Books, 1991.

Miles, William F.S. "Political para-theology: Rethinking religion, politics and democracy". *Third World Quarterly* 17, no. 3 (1996): 525–36.

Milner, Anthony. "Who Created Malaysia's Plural Society?". *Journal of the Malaysian Branch of the Royal Asiatic Society* 72, no. 2 (2003): 1–24.

Moghissi, Haideh. *Feminism and Islamic Fundamentalism: The Limits of Postmodern Analysis*. London: Zed Books, 2002.

Mohamad, Maznah. "Women's Engagement with Political Islam in Malaysia". *Global Change, Peace and Security* 16, no. 2 (2004): 133–49.

Moosa, Ebrahim. "The Dilemma of Islamic Human Rights Schemes". *Journal of Law and Religion* 15, nos. 1–2 (2000–2001): 185–215.

Moten, Abdul Rashid. "Malaysian as an Islamic State: A Political Analysis". *IKIM Journal of Islam and International Affairs* 1, no. 2 (2003): 1–69.

———. "2008 General Election in Malaysia: Democracy at Work". *Japanese Journal of Political Science* 10, no. 1 (2008): 21–42.

Munro-Kua, Anne. *Authoritarian populism in Malaysia*. New York: St Martin's Press, 1996.

Mutalib, Hussin. *Islam and Ethnicity in Malay Politics*. Singapore: Oxford University Press, 1990.

———. *Islam in Malaysia: From Revivalism to Islamic State?* Singapore: Singapore University Press, 1993.

Muzaffar, Chandra. "Malaysia: Islamic Resurgence and the Question of Development". *Sojourn* 1, no. 1 (1986): 57–75.

Nagata, Judith. "Islamic Revival and the Problem of Legitimacy among Rural Religious Elites in Malaysia". *Man* 17, no. 1 (1982): 42–57.

———. *The Reflowering of Malaysian Islam: Modern Religious Radicals and Their Roots*. Vancouver: University of British Columbia Press, 1984.

———. "Ethnonationalism versus Religious Transnationalism: Nation-building and Islam in Malaysia". *The Muslim World* LXXXVII, no. 2 (1997): 129–48.

New Straits Times. "A controversial plan by the Islamic Development Council (JAKIM) to draw up guidelines for live concerts and other musical performances is off — for now". *New Straits Times*, 28 May 2005. <http://www.nst.com.my/Current_News/NST/Saturday/Frontpage/20050528070647/Article/indexb_htm>. Accessed 28 May 2005.

Newby, Gordon D. *A Concise Encyclopedia of Islam*. Oxford: Oneworld, 2002.

Nmehielle, Vincent Obisienunwo Orlu. "Sharia Law in the Northern States of Nigeria: To Implement or Not to Implement, the Constitutionality is the Question". *Human Rights Quarterly* 26, no. 3 (2004): 730–59.

Noor, Farish A. "From Majapahit to Putrajaya: The *Kris* as a Symptom of Civilisation Development and Decline (Part 1)". *Kakiseni.com* 14 January 2002. <http://www.kakiseni.com/articles/columns/MDExMA.html>. Accessed 15 June 2006.

———. "Blood, Sweat and Jihad: The Radicalization of the Political Discourse of the Pan-Malaysian Islamic Party (PAS) from 1982 Onwards". *Contemporary Southeast Asia* 25, no. 2 (2003): 200–32.

———. *Islam Embedded: The Historical Development of the Pan-Malaysian Islamic Party PAS (1951–2003)*. Kuala Lumpur: Malaysian Sociological Research Institute, 2004.

———. "The Battle for Time and Space in Malaysia's Narrowing Society". *Kakiseni.com*, 28 May 2005. <http://www.kakiseni.com/articles/features/MDY3Ng.html>. Accessed 30 May 2005.

————. "'Amok' Season Again: How We Perpetuate the Myths of Empire". *The Other Malaysia*, 18 November 2006. <http://www.othermalaysia.org/content/view/53/48/>. Accessed 9 March 2008.

Norani Othman. "Islamization and democratization in Malaysia in regional and global contexts". In *Challenging Authoritarianism in Southeast Asia*, edited by Ariel Heryanto and Sumit K. Mandal. New York: RoutledgeCurzon, 2004.

Nurul Nazirin. "Controversy over Umno's 'racially provocative' Malays in Peril seminars". *Malaysiakini.com*, 25 March 2005. <http://forum.ipoh.com.my/showthread.php?t=1830>. Accessed 4 April 2009.

Ong, Kian Ming. "Making sense of the political tsunami". *Malaysiakini.com*, 11 March 2008. <http://www.malaysiakini.com/news/79604>. Accessed 11 March 2008.

Ooi Kee Beng, Johan Saravanamuttu, and Lee Hock Guan. *March 8: Eclipsing May 13*. Singapore: Institute of Southeast Asian Studies, 2008.

Osman Bakar. "Islam and political legitimacy in Malaysia". In *Islam and Political Legitimacy*, edited by Shahram Akbarzadeh and Abdullah Saeed. London: RoutledgeCurzon, 2003.

Parti Islam SeMalaysia. *Negara Islam*. Kuala Lumpur: Parti Islam SeMalaysia, 2004. <www.parti-pas.org/IslamicStateDocument.php>. Accessed 18 June 2005.

Peletz, Michael G. "Islam and the Cultural Politics of Legitimacy: Malaysia in the Aftermarth of September 11". In *Remaking Muslim Politics: Pluralism, Contestation, Democracy*, edited by Robert W. Hefner. Princeton: Princeton University Press, 2006.

Pereira, Brendan. "At the Morality Debate, Winners All". *New Straits Times*, 1 May 2005, p. 18.

Phang, L-A. "Don't write serial numbers on ballot papers, EC staff told". *The Sun*, 9 March 2008, p. 10.

Poggi, Gianfranco. *The State: Its Nature, Development and Prospects*. Cambridge: Polity Press, 1990.

Puah, Pauline. "Don't incite Muslims, warns Nazri". *Malaysiakini.com*, 20 March 2006. <http://www.malaysiakini.com/news/48585>. Accessed 14 April 2006.

Puthucheary, Mavis. "Malaysia's Social Contract: Exposing the Myth Behind the Slogan". *Project Malaysia* 1 (2008). <www.projectmalaysia.org/2008/09/malaysias-social-contract-exposing-the-myth-behind-the-slogan/>. Accessed 1 April 2009.

Rappaport, Roy A. *Ritual and Religion in the Making of Humanity*. Cambridge: Cambridge University Press, 1999.

Reed, Jean-Pierre, and John Foran. "Political Cultures of Opposition: Exploring Idioms, Ideologies, and Revolutionary Agency in the Case of Nicaragua". *Critical Sociology* 28, no. 3 (2002): 335–69.

Ricoeur, Paul. *Lectures on Ideology and Utopia*. Edited by George H. Taylor. New York: Columbia University Press, 1986.

Roff, William R. *The Origins of Malay Nationalism*. New Haven: Yale University Press, 1967.

————. "Patterns of Islamization in Malaysia, 1890s–1990s: Exemplars, Institutions, and Vectors". *Journal of Islamic Studies* 9, no. 2 (1998): 210–28.

Salbiah Ahmad. "The freedom of religion impasse and powers of the High Court". *The Journal of the Malaysian Bar* XXXII, no. 3 (2003): 60–90.

————. *Critical Thoughts on Islam, Rights and Freedom in Malaysia*. Petaling Jaya: SIRD, 2007.

Sartre, Jean-Paul. *Literary and Philosophical Essays*. London: Rider and Co., 1955.

————. "Itinerary of a Thought". *New Left Review* 58, no. 9 (1969): 43–66.

Schutz, Alfred. *Alfred Schutz: On Phenomenology and Social Relations*. Edited by Helmut R. Wagner. Chicago: The University of Chicago Press, 1970.

Scott, James. 1985. *Weapons of the Weak: Everyday Forms of Peasant Resistance*. New Haven: Yale University Press, 1985.

————. *Resistance Without Protest: Peasant Opposition to the Zakat in Malaysia and to the Tithe in France. The Fourth James C. Jackson Memorial Lecture, 1986*. Armidale: The University of New England Asia Centre, 1987.

————. "Rituals of Compassion and Social Control". In *Sociology of 'Developing Societies': Southeast Asia*, edited by John G. Taylor and Andrew Turton. London: Macmillan, 1988.

Shahanaaz Habib. "Reject demos and use polls, PM urges public". *The Star*, 10 November 2007, p. N3.

Shamsul, Amri Baharuddin. "A Revival in the Study of Islam". *Man* 18, no. 2 (1983): 399–404.

Sheridan, L.A. and Groves, Harry E. *The Constitution of Malaysia*. 5th ed. Kuala Lumpur: Malayan Law Journal, 2004.

Singh, Hari. "Ethnic Conflict in Malaysia Revisited". *Commonwealth and Comparative Politics* 39, no. 1 (2001): 42–65.

SIS Forum Asia. "Joint Statement: The State Has No Role in Policing Morality". Sisters in Islam, 2005. <http://www.sistersinislam.org.my/MAMP1.htm>. Accessed 15 December 2005.

Stewart, Ian. *The Mahathir Legacy: A Nation Divided, A Region at Risk*. Crows Nest: Allen and Unwin, 2003.

Syed Ahmad Hussein. "Muslim Politics and the Discourse on Democracy". In *Democracy in Malaysia: Discourses and Practices*, edited by Khoo Boo Teik and Francis Loh Kok Wah. Richmond: Curzon, 2002.

Syed Akbar Ali. *Things in Common*. Kuala Lumpur: Syed Akbar Ali, 2008.

Syed Husin Ali. "The changing faces of politics and repression in Malaysia". *Inter-Asia Cultural Studies* 2, no. 1 (2001): 115–26.

————. "Authoritarian State, Ethnic Violence and Our Tasks". In *Out of the Tempurung: Critical Essays on Malaysian Society*, edited by Fong Chin Wei and Yin Ee Kiong. Sydney: East West Publishing, 2008*a*.

————. *The Malays: Their Problems and Future*. Kuala Lumpur: The Other Press, 2008*b*.

Syed Naguib Al-Attas. *Preliminary Statement on a General Theory of the Islamization of the Malay-Indonesian Archipelago*. Kuala Lumpur: Dewan Bahasa dan Pustaka, 1969.

Tajfel, Henri. "Experiments in Intergroup Discrimination". *Scientific American* 232, no. 2 (1970): 92–102.

Tan Eng Kong and John E. Carr. "Psychiatric Sequelae of Amok". *Culture, Medicine and Psychiatry* 1, no. 1 (1977): 59–67.

Tan, Jason. "Law and religious order: The court of Tuan Haji Sulaiman Abdullah". *Off The Edge* 31 (2007): 38–45.

Teh Yik Koon. "Mak Nyahs (Male Trannssexuals) in Malaysia: The Influence of Culture and Religion on their Identity". *The International Journal of Transgenderism* 5, no. 3 (2001). <http://www.symposion.com/ijt/ijtvo05no03_04.htm>.

Theophilus, Claudia. "Orang Asli cry foul over 'forced' conversion". *Malaysiakini. com*, 3 February 2005. <http://www.malaysiakini.com/news/33358>. Accessed 3 October 2006.

————. "Public reminder to uphold constitutional supremacy". *Malaysiakini.com*, 16 March 2006*a*. <http://www.malaysiakini.com/news/48253>. Accessed 14 April 2006.

————. "Police ignored mob, say forum organisers". *Malaysiakini.com*, 15 May 2006*b*. <http://www.malaysiakini.com/news/51087>. Accessed 3 October 2006.

The Sun. "14 Islamic NGOs to stage religious forum on Saturday". *The Sun*, 8 August 2006. <http://www.sun2surf.com/article.cfm?id=15036>. Accessed 10 September 2006.

Toth, James. "Local Islam Gone Global: The Roots of Religious Militancy in Egypt and its Transnational Transformation". In *Social Movements: An Anthropological Reader*, edited by June Nash. Oxford: Blackwell Publishing, 2002.

Transparency International. *Global Corruption Report 2008: Corruption in the Water Sector*. Cambridge: Cambridge University Press, 2008.

Turnbull, Mary C. *A History of Malaysia, Singapore and Brunei*. Hong Kong: Allen and Unwin, 1989.

van Dijk, Kees. "The good, the bad and the ugly: Explaining the unexplainable: amuk massa in Indonesia". In *Roots of Violence in Indonesia*, edited by Freek Colombijn and J. Thomas Lindblad. Singapore: Institute of Southeast Asian Studies, 2002.

————. "National Pride and Foreign Influences: The Evolution of Mosque Design in Malaysia and Indoneisa". In *The Malaysian Way of Life*, edited by Julian C.H. Lee. Shah Alam: Marshall Cavendish, 2010.

Volpi, Frédéric and Cavatora, Francesco. "Forgetting Democratization? Recasting Power and Authority in a Plural Muslim World". *Democratization* 13, no. 3 (2006): 363–72.

Waldron, Jeremy. "The Constitutional Conception of Democracy". In *Democracy*, edited by David Estlund. Oxford: Blackwell Publishers, 2002.

Watson, C.W. *Of Self and Nation: Autobiography and the Representation of Modern Indonesia*. Honolulu: University of Hawai'i Press, 2000.

Weiss, Meredith L. "The 1999 Malaysian General Elections: Issues, Insults, and Irregularities". *Asian Survey* 40, no. 3 (2000): 413–35.

―――. "The Malaysian Human Rights Movement". In *Social Movements in Malaysia: From moral communities to NGOs*, edited by Meredith L. Weiss and Saliha Hassan. London: RoutledgeCurzon, 2004.

Weiss, Meredith L. and Saliha Hassan. "Introduction: From moral communities to NGOs". In *Social Movements in Malaysia: From moral communities to NGOs*, edited by Meredith L. Weiss and Saliha Hassan. London: RoutledgeCurzon, 2004.

Welsh, Bridget. "Higher education crisis deepening?". *Malaysiakini.com*, 10 August 2005. <http://www.malaysiakini.com/opinionsfeatures/38832>. Accessed 15 August 2005.

Wolf, Eric R. "Facing Power — Old Insights, New Questions". In *The Anthropology of Politics: A Reader in Ethnography, Theory and Critique*, edited by Joan Vincent. Oxford: Blackwell Publishers, 2002.

Wong Chin Huat. "The federal and state elections in Malaysia, March 2004". *Electoral Studies* 24, no. 2 (2005): 311–19.

Wong, Elizabeth. "Officers asked for women's phone numbers". *Malaysiakini.com*, 7 February 2005. <http://www.malaysiakini.com/letters/33464>. Accessed 8 February 2005.

Wu Min Aun. *The Malaysian Legal System*. 2nd ed. Petaling Jaya: Longman, 1999.

Young, Iris Marion. "Communication and the Other: Beyond Deliberative Democracy". In *Democracy and Difference: Contesting the Boundaries of the Political*, edited by Seyla Benhabib. Princeton: Princeton University Press, 1996.

Zainah Anwar. *Islamic revivalism in Malaysia: Dakwah among the students*. Petaling Jaya: Pelanduk Publications, 1987.

―――. "Law-Making in the Name of Islam". In *Islam in Southeast Asia: Political, Social and Strategic Challenges for the 21ˢᵗ Century*, edited by K.S. Nathan and Mohammad Hashim Kamali. Singapore: Institute of Southeast Asian Studies, 2005.

Zartman, I. William. "Islam, the State, and Democracy: The Contradictions". In *Between the State and Islam*, edited by Charles E. Butterworth and I. William Zartman. Cambridge: Cambridge University Press, 2001.

INDEX

Medina, 18, 52, 59
Mehmet, Ozay, 15
Melaka (state), 91, 131
Merleau-Ponty, Maurice, 30, 32
Mernissi, Fatima, 102
MIC (Malaysian Indian Congress),
    40, 112
Middle East, 19, 21, 36, 102
Miles, William F.S., 20
Milne, R.S., 17
Milner, Anthony, 37, 44
Ministry of Information, 52, 119
Moghissi, Haideh, 18
Mohamad, Maznah, 100
Mohamad Rahmat, 47
Mohamad Ya, 87
Mohamed Ariff Yusof, 74–76, 77
Mohamed Hakim case, 69
Mohamed Nazri Aziz, 27
Moorthy, M., 93, 94, 128
Moosa, Ebrahim, 17
Moten, Abdul Rashid, 55–56, 58, 130
Muhammad, Prophet, 52, 98–99, 104
Muhammad Abu Zuhrah, Syaikh, 52
Muhammad bin Hasan Al-Syaibani,
    53
Muhammad Ridzan Mogarajah,
    84–85, 91
Munro-Kua, Anne, 41, 46
Muslim Brotherhood, 23–24
*Muslim Women and the Challenges of
    Islamic Extremism*, 14
Muslim Youth Movement of Malaysia,
    see Angkatan Belia Islam Malaysia
Mutalib, Hussin, 39, 50n1
Muzaffar, Chandra, 15–16, 122
Myanmar, 26

N
Nagata, Judith, 16, 17, 50n1, 60, 100
Najib Tun Razak, 45, 49
National Fatwa Council, 73n4, 132,
    133, 134

National Human Rights Society, 105
National Mosque, 48
National Operations Council, 42
National Registration Department
    (NRD), 63, 64, 70
Negeri Sembilan, 131
Netherlands, 12, 36
New Economic Policy (NEP), 42–43
New Era College, 122
New Straits Times, 49, 95, 131n2
New Yorker, The, 108n2
Newby, Gordon, 80
Newsweek, 117
Nicaragua, 21–22
Nicholas, Colin, 34
Nigeria, 96
Nik Adli Nik Aziz, 23
Nik Aziz Nik Mat, 23
Nik Noriani, 101, 102
1969 riots, 40–42, 43–47, 94, 118
niqaab, 12
Nmehielle, Vincent Obisienunwo
    Orlu, 96
non-governmental organizations, 27,
    48, 84, 91, 116
    see also Article 11 coalition;
    Malaysians Against Moral
    Policing; Sisters in Islam
non-Muslims
    Constitution and, 66
    freedom of religion, 87–89, 128–29
    intimidation of, 77–78
    Mahathir's policies and, 16
    marginalization, 32, 55, 59, 95
    objection to Islamic statehood, 52,
        56, 75
    PAS and, 113
    place in nation, 9
    Syariah law and, 54, 84, 93–94, 96
Noor, Farish A., 16, 23, 43, 47, 50n1,
    94
Norani Othman, 14
North Africa, 21

ABOUT THE AUTHOR

Julian C.H. Lee is a lecturer in the School of Arts and Social Sciences at Monash University. He was recently an Economic and Social Research Council (ESRC) Postdoctoral Fellow in the School of Anthropology and Conservation at the University of Kent. He is the editor of *The Malaysian Way of Life* (2010) and his articles have appeared in journals including *Anthropological Forum, Anthropology Today, Development, Social Movement Studies, The Round Table* and *Südostasien Aktuell.*

Lee is also a regular contributor to the Malaysian arts and culture magazine, *Off The Edge,* and is also the magazine's wine columnist.

1. A poster photographed on the grounds of a church depicting Malaysia's first Prime Minister, Tunku Abdul Rahman.

2. Zaitun "Toni" Kasim discussing Quranic verse 24:4.

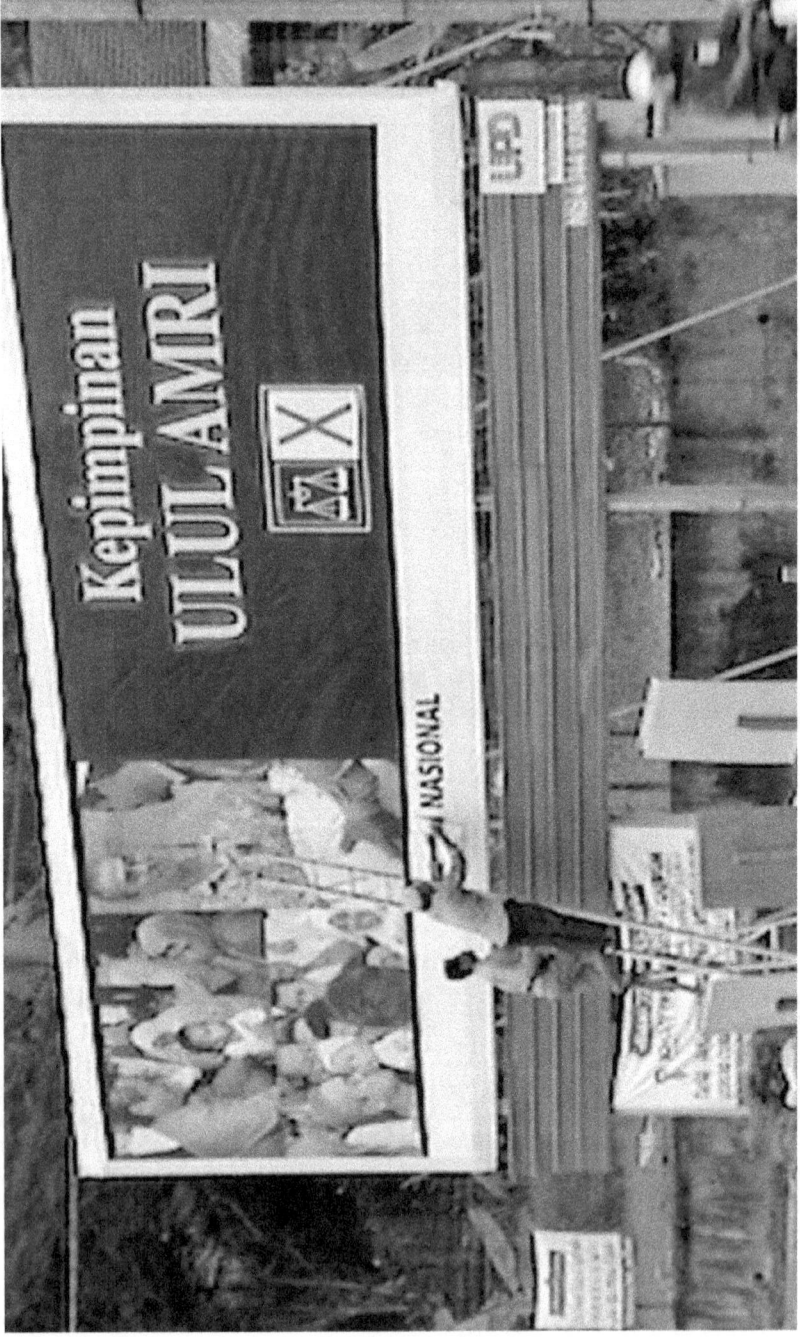

3. Workers covering up the phrase "*Pilihan yang Bijak: Barisan Nasional*" (The Smart Choice: National Front).

4. A PKR *pondok panas* set up on 8 March 2008, polling day.

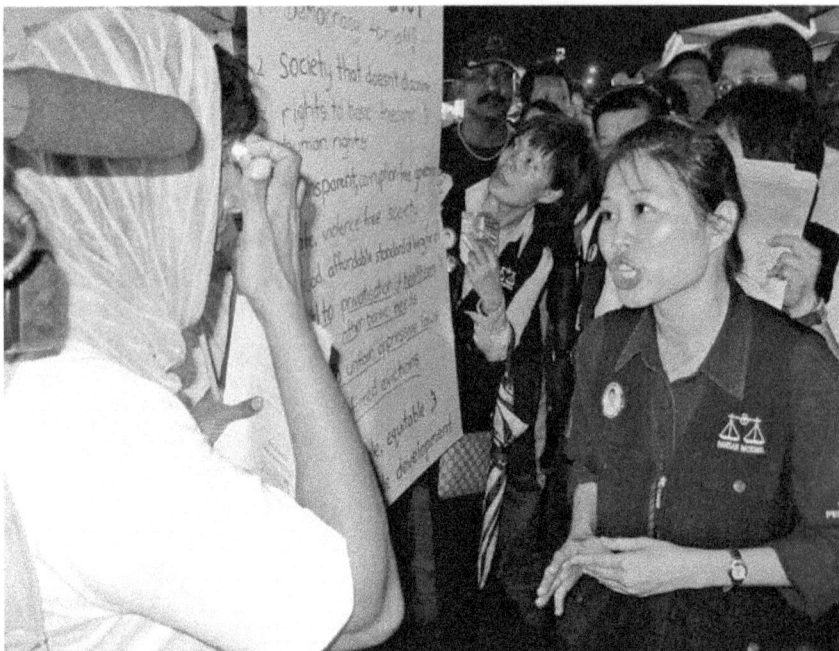

5. Mak Bedah speaking to MCA candidate in 2008 elections, Carol Chew.

6. A demonstrator at the Bersih demonstration on 10 November 2007 in front of a police personnel vehicle.

7. Part of the Bersih demonstration in Kuala Lumpur.

MEW CHOO WINS CHINA OPEN
>> BACK PAGE

THREE MALAYSIAN WOMEN FACE DEATH PENALTY IN PAKISTAN
>> P9

DEFIANCE

IT was an illegal assembly. A permit had been denied; a court injunction obtained. The warnings had been clear.

Yesterday in Kuala Lumpur, several thousand Hindraf supporters (estimates range from 5,000 by the police to 10,000 by the local and foreign press) defied those orders. For the second time in two weeks, water cannon sprayed and tear gas billowed over crowds of protesters. But the cause for which they rallied — a demand of RM28 trillion in reparations from the British government for historical exploitation of Indians — ended in clashes with the police.

Shops closed and normally busy streets were almost deserted as a result. And it ended without the group presenting the memorandum to the British High Commission.

A protester throws back a tear gas canister at riot police during the demonstration in Kuala Lumpur yesterday. — AFP picture

[REPORTS & PIX: P2-7]

8. The front page of the *New Straits Times* on 26 November 2007. The main image depicts a demonstrator hurling a tear gas canister. The headline reads "*Defiance*".

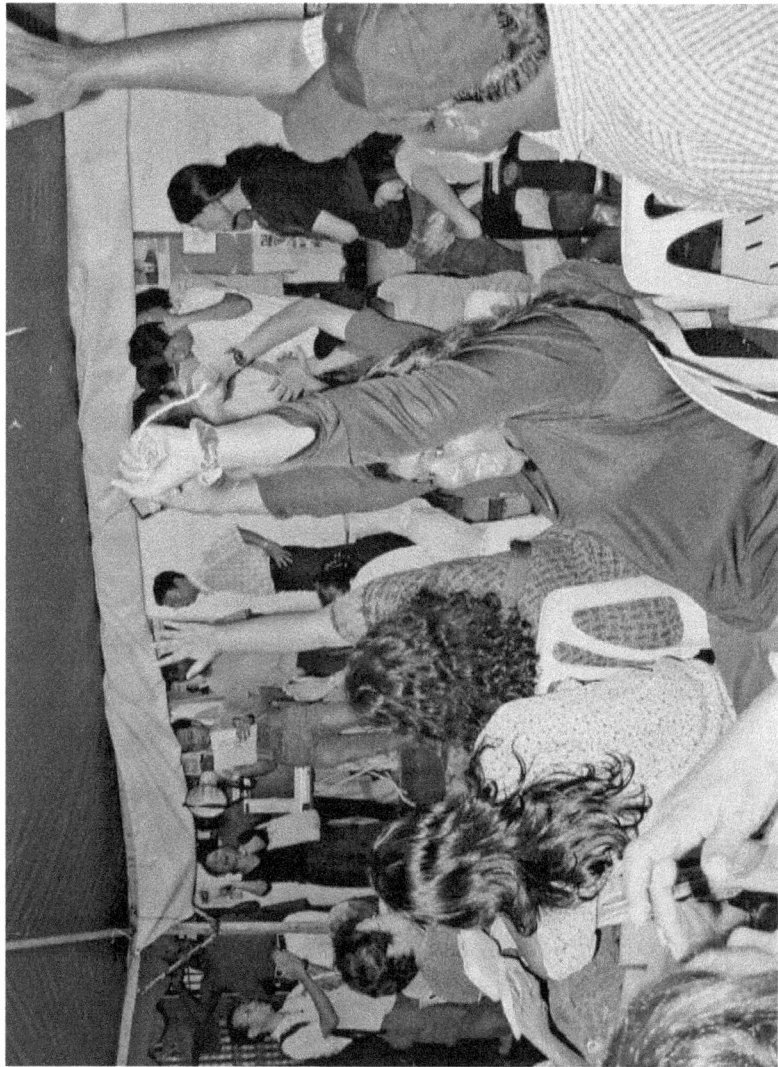

9. Supporters of PKR candidate Sivarasa Rasiah celebrating as results of the elections came in on polling night, 8 March 2008.

www.ingramcontent.com/pod-product-compliance
Lightning Source LLC
Chambersburg PA
CBHW020751300326
41914CB00050B/89